MENTORING TEACHI

Mentoring Teachers provides practical guidance for teacher mentors, directly addressing common queries and concerns they may have while acting as a mentor within a diverse range of educational contexts. Drawing upon the author's 30 years of conducting research on mentoring and working with both experienced and new mentors, this essential book provides a detailed picture of the mentoring role.

Dividing the mentor role into five key aspects (Support, Acculturator, Model, Sponsor and Educator), this important resource provides step-by-step descriptions of managing mentorials in ways which:

- support the mentor in scaffolding a mentee's thinking so that they can make their own informed judgements and decisions about teaching;
- develop the mentee's noticing skills for responsive, adaptive teaching;
- guide the mentee towards recognising the relevance of others' ideas or 'theories' to their own practice and experience;
- leave the mentee with practical ideas and plans for teaching and developing their teaching skills; and
- scaffold the mentee's learning of Systematic Informed Reflective Practice (SIRP) to support their ongoing learning and development by themselves.

Mentoring can, if effective, contribute to mentees' learning, wellbeing and retention in the profession. *Mentoring Teachers* describes effective mentoring practice and is a crucial read for any mentor, aspiring mentor or mentor programme co-ordinator.

Angi Malderez has 30 years' experience in mentoring, running mentor preparation and ongoing support programmes and providing support to others who are establishing or running such mentoring schemes in various countries worldwide, all while herself learning and developing from these experiences. She has also conducted a range of formal research, including as co-director of a six-year longitudinal study, the Becoming a Teacher (BaT) project, and as consultant on subsequent mentoring research projects.

MENTORING TEACHERS

Supporting Learning, Wellbeing and Retention

Angi Malderez

Routledge
Taylor & Francis Group

LONDON AND NEW YORK

First published 2024
by Routledge
4 Park Square, Milton Park, Abingdon, Oxon OX14 4RN

and by Routledge
605 Third Avenue, New York, NY 10158

Routledge is an imprint of the Taylor & Francis Group, an informa business

British Library Cataloguing-in-Publication Data
A catalogue record for this book is available from the British Library

ISBN: 978-1-032-55095-4 (hbk)
ISBN: 978-1-032-55094-7 (pbk)
ISBN: 978-1-003-42900-5 (ebk)

DOI: 10.4324/9781003429005

Typeset in Interstate
by Apex CoVantage, LLC

Dedicated to Mentors of Teachers everywhere

Who, often despite a lack of (sufficient) preparation and support for their own development, undertake, on top of their own teaching, this most vital of roles.

CONTENTS

ACKNOWLEDGEMENTS

Four people provided their invaluable perspectives on the drafts of this book as it evolved, and helped me enrich and improve the text. They are Elena Oncevska Ager, Anna Szegedy-Maszák, Caroline Bodóczky and my son Gary Hernandez. Perhaps most importantly, they provided the love, encouragement, support and nudging I needed to finally get it done. Without them, this book would not be here. A huge thank you from me – for your belief in me and persuading me that the book is needed and worthwhile and for not letting me give up. They each, in my mind, had specific roles.

Elena, a former student, now a friend and a Teacher of Teachers (ToT), always responded promptly to requests for comments on chapters. Over the seven or eight years it has taken me to bring this project to fruition, she has helped me crystalise my thoughts on the book during our frequent video-calls and message exchanges, and, when energy and enthusiasm flagged, encouraged me to "just write it!"

Anna, as a practising school-based mentor and new mentor trainer, provided, in her thoughtful and thought-provoking comments on drafts, invaluable insights into the current challenges in her context. She also persuaded me of the need for this book.

Caroline, a dear friend, erstwhile colleague and co-author, not only co-created our original non-judgemental approach, but also introduced me to Anna and read and commented on drafts. Her voice was also in my head as I edited and crafted my writing, chiding me, for example, on "another one" of my "back-to-front sentences!" Phone conversations with her also helped me clarify and confirm my thoughts about how parts of this developed approach, as it is depicted here, might be challenging for some readers in some contexts.

I'd not only like to acknowledge the general filial support my son Gary provides, but also to thank him for the many conversations about an in-service mentoring scheme he was planning to set up in a UK higher education (HE) context, and for providing the opportunity to do some face-to-face training work with him and his colleagues who were becoming mentors. These very recent experiences have helped me confirm my view on the suitability of this approach in such HE contexts where, in the UK at least, mentoring schemes may exist, but are aimed at career or research development, rather than at the professional development of teachers and their teaching. I also gained an extra impetus to 'get the book done.' In addition, the memory of him working, daily and diligently, on his master's thesis has inspired me to overcome my procrastination and do at least *some* 'book-work' every day.

A big thank you, too, to my friend and colleague Doina Fleanta, who in the midst of a very busy and demanding personal-professional life, responded promptly to my request for her story in mentoring.

Next, I'd like to thank the anonymous reviewers of my book proposal to the publishers for their positive reviews and for the suggestions and perspectives that have, I hope, improved the book.

I'd like also to acknowledge the importance of and influence on the development of the approach described in this book of others I have worked with in the past. Firstly, I am hugely grateful to all the mentors worldwide who have attended the courses I have given for the challenges we overcame and the learning we shared. Two former colleagues also deserve a special mention. The first of these is Professor Medgyes Peter, who gave me my first job in mentoring which was to establish, with Caroline, the teaching experience strand of our Initial Teacher Preparation (ITP) programme at CETT (Centre for English Teacher Training) Eötvos Lòrand University in Budapest. More recently, working as a co-researcher and co-author with Professor A.J. Hobson was both enlightening and rewarding, and his friendship and current research publications continue to inspire me. I owe a huge debt of gratitude to both.

Finally, I'd like to send my thanks to all those involved in the emergence of this book in its tangible form: in particular to Bruce Roberts, my editor, for having faith in the project and to Lauren Readhead, assistant editor for her empathic care, excellent communication skills and patience. Finally, my thanks to my wonderful cover designer Jo Steer and to Jeff Malderez, my other son, who not only contributed via his personal support to me, but also via his artistic talents which helped me show Jo the kind of thing I had in mind.

My sincere thanks to you all. It really does take a village to raise a book!

Introduction and definitions

Reading and writing can be seen as engaging in a kind of 'dialogue-at-a-distance.' Any conversation is smoother when the participants know each other, at least a bit. This is why I am beginning this introductory chapter by explaining a bit about myself and outlining who I imagine you, the readers, are. I go on to describe what this book is and what it is not before discussing the whys: why I wrote the book and why you might want to read it. Next, I explain what I mean by the term mentoring and outline the model of mentoring used in the book. I do so because I have come across so many different ways of understanding what mentoring is. Without this explanation, our conversation may falter. I also briefly outline why I think you, mentors, have a crucial and irreplaceable role to play in supporting teacher learning and wellbeing, which in turn enhance retention. Next, before I write a few words about language, there is a section which looks briefly at the notion of 'help' in relation to mentoring. This introductory chapter continues with a description of the book itself in the form of summaries of what is in each chapter, and it ends with some ideas on how you might want to use the book.

Who am I, the author?

I am a teacher. That's my first answer to that question. I have taught groups of people of various ages, from children to adults. Those people were with me to learn things ranging from school subjects (mainly languages) to teaching, mentoring and supporting the learning of teaching more generally (teaching teaching). I have undertaken research in the fields of teacher learning and mentoring while in a formal academic role, but my identity has always been as a teacher. By teacher, by the way, I do not mean 'teller' or someone who 'delivers a course' but rather someone who is, or tries to be, a supporter of learning, and who sees a 'course' as a process that evolves in real time between particular people in a particular context. Most knowledge or learning cannot be 'delivered' or handed over like a parcel, and it is dangerous to believe that it can. As I have just revealed, I am also someone who cares a lot about what I see as the unhelpful language metaphors, such as 'delivering a course', commonly used in education these days. What else would it be helpful for you to know? Well, I have been fortunate to work with mentors in many parts of the world (from Chile to China, Romania to Rwanda and Estonia to Ethiopia), and I have made mentoring the main focus

DOI: 10.4324/9781003429005-1

of my work for more than three decades. I would say I am passionate about mentoring. Apart from that, I am a proud mother and grandmother.

Who are you, the reader?

I am writing this book primarily for teachers becoming, or already also acting as, mentors. When I write 'you' in this book, I mean you-mentor (or you-mentor-to-be). You might be, for example:

- engaged in partnerships with higher education colleagues which support people working towards their first teaching qualifications. These qualifications often, but not always, function as a license-to-teach and must be obtained before starting a career. Your mentor role in such partnerships is to support the learning-in-school of a student preparing to be a qualified teacher;
- working with an already qualified teacher colleague wanting support for his/her ongoing development as a teacher as a normal part of being a professional; or
- working with a colleague within a strategy of support, perhaps in a context where there is a new top-down mandated educational reform.

You might be a school-based mentor, that is, a teacher in the same school or institution as your mentee. On the other hand, you might be an external mentor, that is, a fellow teacher of the same subject working in a different school or institution, and often mentoring online.

You may work informally, meaning no one has asked you to take on this role apart from your mentee, or be formally tasked with the role as part of a larger scheme. If you are working formally, you may or may not be actually called a mentor in your system (and not all those people called 'mentors' do actually mentor – see below). However, if you are working one-to-one with a colleague with the express aim of supporting that colleague's wellbeing and professional development, you are, in my terms, a mentor. A requirement to mentor may be part of your job description. If this is not the case, you may have volunteered for this role, as a way, perhaps, of remaining engaged in, or of giving something back to, the profession. Perhaps you volunteered in order to learn something new – and research has indeed established (Hobson et al., 2009) that mentors of beginning teachers do learn about teaching as well as about mentoring from their engagement in mentoring relationships. So, I see you, teachers who have also taken on the role of being a mentor for a colleague, as my main readership.

Others who might be interested in this book include:

- those running programmes aimed at preparing qualified teachers, as well as
- those running related MA courses;

- those involved in setting up and providing the conditions for proposed mentoring schemes who might find the details here informative and relevant; and finally,
- those devising programmes to support mentor development. The book may help someone running such a programme to clarify their thinking, or suggest ideas for mentor development programme content, for example. However, I should hate it if parts of it became the basis for long 'delivered' lectures. Why do I say that? I believe that just as people cannot and do not become teachers simply by being told things, so teachers do not and cannot become mentors through simply being told things (see Chapters 6 and 8 in particular). If they are just 'told things' they are likely to do the same, inappropriately, with their mentees (and see 'Why I have written this book' below).

What this book is (and what it is not)

This book is a handbook for mentors. It is a handbook in that it describes practical ways of acting as a mentor which have resulted in effective mentoring in various contexts. So, what do I mean by effective mentoring? For me, being 'effective' as a mentor means working in such a way that it supports mentees' learning of teaching and of reflective practice, their wellbeing and their chances of remaining in and being committed to the profession. These outcomes – learning, wellbeing and retention – are ones that research has found are the potential benefits of effective mentoring (and explain the book's subtitle).

To some extent, what counts as effective depends on the context and the goals set. Most systems I know require a mentor to support a mentee's *learning* of teaching. This requirement is usually visible through the stated aim for or definition of mentoring in any system. In addition, many, if not most, systems and programmes aim for a *professional* workforce and may explicitly associate being a *reflective practitioner* with this aim. For me, being a reflective practitioner *is* a part of being professional (see Chapter 4). Managerially, policy-makers in some systems (particularly those in the global North) are concerned to stem the tide of teacher dropout and have identified mentoring as a strategy that can, if effective, support job satisfaction and retention (Hobson et al., 2009).

As well as being a practical handbook with descriptions of things mentors say to or do with and for their mentees, this book also includes some background ideas, some 'theory.' This is because, in mentoring as in teaching, what matters is not so much what practitioners do (although we do have to *have* things to do) as *why* we do it. The general answers to the big 'why' in both cases is 'because it's what my mentee/pupils need now', or 'it helps my mentee/pupils take the next steps on their learning journey.' One of my favourite axioms is 'a teacher's responsibility is his/her response-ability' – our duty is to respond to the learning needs of our pupils. So it is with mentors. Developing 'response-ability' as a mentor requires many things, including the ability to notice signs of need, having a clear idea of the learning processes we are supporting and having something to *do* to respond (the practical ideas) and the skills to implement them. Throughout the chapters of this book, therefore, you will find sections of what I like to call *practical* theory in conjunction with the descriptions of things that mentors do. These ideas are 'practical' because they are ones that I and the mentors I have worked with have found useful in developing our own response-ability.

There are a number of things this book is not or does not do. It does not, for example, suggest a list of things that mentees *should* learn. Apart from the fact that every mentee is different and will realise the need to learn different things at different times, contexts vary in their expectations of what it is that teachers should know. Furthermore, the book is not a prescription. It is not 'right', although it is informed and as up to date as I can make it at the time of writing. Nor does it represent, for example, an accurate depiction of any one mentor's practice – reality is a lot messier than would be acceptable in a book. Above all, it is not enough to prepare a teacher-becoming-mentor. As well as *knowing about* (see below), what I describe in the book, you, if you are new to mentoring, will need experiences and time to develop the skills to use the ideas and practices presented here. So, do be as patient with yourself as you are or will be with your mentee!

I trust, however, that this book does present a coherent informed idea of what some effective mentors do and what being an effective mentor might be like.

Why I have written this book

I was encouraged to write this book largely by mentors I have worked with (thank you). I expect, however, that it is clear from what I have written so far that I believe a book is no substitute for experiential initial preparation and development opportunities for teachers becoming and being mentors. I also believe that, to be effective, these development opportunities need to be of sufficient duration and regularity. In the early 1990s, my colleague and friend Caroline and I were developing our approach to supporting initial mentor preparation. Our book describing this was published in 1999 (Malderez and Bodòczky). It is still my preferred approach in mentor training, and I still use many, even most, of the activities and processes included in it and draw on ideas developed or found at that time. There have, however, been some changes in the way I work, born of my experiences and learning over the years, and supported by the invaluable daily 'reactions' and the subsequent experiences of the many course participants I have worked with. Some of these changes have, for example, to do with the language I use – for example, being very careful about when or even whether I ever use the term 'feedback' (see Chapter 6). Another is that I include many more metaphorical stories (see Chapter 9 for some examples and Chapter 8, Modes of Mind, for a theoretical rationale). The final and most important change concerns the mentorial protocols I now propose, spend considerable course time on and use in mentorial role-plays (see Chapter 6). From the start, we had realised that a non-judgemental approach to mentoring was essential in order to ensure the safe, trusting context of the mentor–mentee relationship. We had also, however, drawn from the sparse literature on mentoring teachers from the 1980s and taken the 'mentor' practices of 'observation and providing feedback' as a given. It very soon became clear as we all struggled to remain non-judgemental that we had a problem. I went back to what it might mean to support teacher *learning* (see Malderez and Wedell, 2007, and below) and the developed approach to mentoring described in this book is the result.

So, while I hope you are reading this alongside or in conjunction with such a face-to-face experiential mentor development programme, most contexts I know do not, perhaps only as yet, provide such favourable conditions for mentor development. I am hoping that you can find support in this book to manage your own development, and perhaps increase that support by working with another colleague to practise skills needed, (for example, in the use of mentorial protocols, or for developing your own listening skills) as well to discuss ideas in chapters.

My other reasons for finally deciding to write the book relate to the current context of mentoring worldwide and recent developments and research I have read or undertaken. I briefly describe three of these here. The first relates to what we now know about effective mentoring. Summarising the outcomes of a number of studies (including his own, some of which I was involved in) Professor A.J. Hobson (editor of the *International Journal of Mentoring and Coaching in Education*) describes effective mentoring as being ONSIDE (2016). Apart from expressing the idea that effective mentors are 'on the side' of their mentees, the acronym stands for:

- **O**ff-line, meaning it is different and separated from line management or supervision and is non-hierarchical;
- **N**on-evaluative and non-judgemental, leaving the space for mentees to learn to make their own informed judgements and decisions;
- **S**upportive of mentees' wellbeing and psychosocial needs;
- **I**ndividualised and tailored to the specific and changing needs (emotional and developmental) of each mentee;
- **D**evelopmental and growth oriented, promoting mentees' 'learnacy' (see Chapter 6); and
- **E**mpowering and enabling mentees to become autonomous.

Enabling mentoring to be ONSIDE requires, ideally, the provision of certain conditions (see Chapter 1). The understanding and informed vision of many people in any one system are needed if these conditions are to be provided or enabled. These people include, for example, policy-makers, providers of programmes leading to teaching qualifications/certification, headteachers, as well as the mentors themselves. However, the provision of ideal conditions takes time (and other resources) to effect. Meanwhile, it is you, existing mentors, who need, on a daily basis, to have things to do and a way of being and thinking which allows you to remain ONSIDE, and, crucially, to do so whatever your context. This book attempts to help you do that.

Secondly, Professor Hobson and I re-analysed some of the data related specifically to mentoring that we had generated in an earlier large-scale study (The Becoming a Teacher study, Hobson et al., 2009). What we found, apart from ample evidence that effective mentoring was valuable, were many reports of a phenomenon we termed "judgementoring" (Hobson and Malderez, 2013). This occurred when a mentor revealed their own evaluations of and judgements on a mentee's teaching and in so doing jeopardised the safe relationship – did not remain ONSIDE – and rendered their work ineffective at best and at worst contributed to the mentee drop-out. Given other data from our study and those of others, we traced some of the probable causes of judgementoring back to:

- the mentors' own prior experiences learning teaching;
- a lack of sufficient appropriate opportunities for mentor development, leaving a mentor with no or few alternative options to judgementoring practices; and
- a requirement to take on the conflicting non-mentor duties of assessing mentees (see Chapter 7).

Since publishing our paper, we have heard from people in many other countries who recognised judgementoring as a phenomenon in their systems too. This has worried me a lot. I know and believe that teacher mentoring has an important role to play in any education system. Just *how* important I try to explain below. However, if judgementoring persists, what happens when the policy-makers and those with the power to create the more favourable conditions that support effective mentoring hear of the negative effects of judgementoring? They might, if they do not make the distinction between judgementoring and mentoring, give up on the idea of a mentoring scheme or supporting mentoring altogether. So, I have a mission to do what I can to ensure that all mentors, whatever their context, have access to ways of avoiding judgementoring and remaining ONSIDE. This book is part of that effort. In particular, Chapter 6 provides a non-judgemental way of dealing with post-lesson discussions, and Chapter 7 proposes a safer, mentoring way to combine both assessor and mentor duties, in contexts where this is still necessary.

Finally, as mentoring spreads, some systems have begun developing mentor standards which, it is proposed, mentors can or should aspire to. This raises two issues. The first is when the standards seem to promote, or include language that suggests judgementoring practices as a given. The second relates to how you might provide evidence of achievement of any explicit mentor standards in your context (when/if required to) while still remaining ONSIDE, which this book also touches on (see Chapters 1 and 6).

Why you might want to read this book

It follows from what I have written so far that I think you might want to read this book if you have recently decided (or are required or expected) to undertake the role of a mentor.

If you are a more-experienced mentor, you might find this book especially useful if you have had few or no opportunities for your own development as a mentor. Others of you may find ways forward when faced with specific dilemmas, such as, how to avoid or minimise judgementoring when faced with the requirement to also take on the non-mentor duties of formally assessing your mentee and disclosing the results; or how you might support a mentee who just doesn't seem to notice some of the effects of what they do in class; or how to work with a mentee planning for and preparing to teach a lesson.

The view of teacher mentoring in this book

The first thing to say is that my view of teacher mentoring, which I shall first attempt to describe as briefly as I can here and exemplify in more detail throughout this book, is an informed one. I have been informed by, amongst other experiences, my reading of authors writing about mentoring and teacher learning, my engagement in research about teacher learning and the role of others in those processes (including mentors), as well as my own lived experience and learning as a mentor and while working with both teachers becoming mentors and with experienced mentors.

You have picked up this book, and so you already have a view on mentoring, though you may or may not have ever put that view into words. I present my own view here for two main reasons. The first is to try to ensure we are talking about the same thing or so that you can discover where our views may seem to differ. The second is to explain something about why the book is organised as it is.

Mentoring, in the teaching profession, is the support given by one teacher for the wellbeing and learning of another and for his or her integration into the cultures of the school and the wider profession. There, that's a short academic definition. But as a teacher, a practitioner, I need to be able to imagine what that looks like in practice. I wonder whether, on reading that last sentence and in order to build a vision and to see it in practice, you began to remember occasions when another teacher worked one to one with you? If so, can I ask you to 'park' those memories, to put them to one side for the moment? I ask this because the teacher who worked with you may have been acting as a trainer, supervisor or assessor (whatever their title) rather than enacting one or more of the five roles of a mentor (and see Table 0.1 below).

An effective mentor – one who does in fact support the wellbeing and learning of the mentee and his or her integration into the cultures of the school and the wider profession – fulfils five roles. I will mention these roles only briefly here because, although they do add to the definition and explain why the book is organised as it is, each is described in much more detail later in the book (see Chapters 2 to 6). Having an understanding of mentor roles will also help you when undertaking the preparatory task in Chapter 1. I present them here in the order they are introduced in the book. I chose this order because, despite the fact that all roles are important in my view (although they will need more or less emphasis in particular contexts and with particular mentees), some need more or special attention at particular stages of all mentoring processes. Here they are. You, as a mentor have:

- a Support role – supporting the mentee as a person through the emotional roller coaster that learning teaching often entails;
- an Acculturator role – helping the mentee adjust to, integrate into, and contribute to the cultures of the school and the wider profession;
- a Model role – modelling professionalism and a way of being and learning as a teacher;
- a Sponsor role – using any knowledge or contacts you have to help your mentee; and
- an Educator role – helping the mentee learn teaching and learn to learn teaching.

In some systems, for example, in England, people talk about 'mentoring *and* coaching.' But if I take Elaine Cox's definition of coaching as "facilitated reflective practice" (2012), then coaching is and always has been, in this model of mentoring (see Malderez, 2004), a *part* of mentoring and perhaps the main practice in the core Educator role (and see Table 0.2 below and Chapter 6).

I feel I can hear some of you thinking, "Ok, that helped a bit but it's still all rather theoretical and I still can't see clearly what it means in practice." Well, that's what this whole book is about really, but perhaps it might help here if I list some of the things mentors do and don't do. If you began to remember your own experiences at the start of this section, you might like to compare them with the lists below.

What mentors do

A Martian visiting a school with a mentor–mentee relationship in progress would need to look very closely to spot what a mentor does. In fact, the Martian might only notice that the mentor spends as much time with the mentee as with any other colleague, if not more, and that mentor and mentee spend most of their time together talking. The Martian might also notice that the mentee talks proportionately much more than the mentor.

From the point of view of the mentor, some of the things mentors may be doing are as follows:

- making their own professional learning processes visible (Model role).
- providing information on how/when/where to carry out school requirements (Acculturator role).
- encouraging, listening and maybe on occasion doing things FOR the mentee (Support role).
- lending the mentee a book or materials (Sponsor role).
- guiding a process based on a lesson their mentee has taught, so that their mentee develops noticing skills which enable them to take account of pupil reactions and feedback, and listening attentively so that the mentee can make *his or her own* judgements and decisions (Educator role).

What mentors do not do, as a rule (but judgementors DO do)

- Observe a mentee's teaching and 'give feedback' (meaning 'assess' – see Chapter 7).
- Give advice (almost always assessment-based, too) about how to teach.

So, if you compared your initial ideas with what I have just written, was there a mismatch? I wouldn't be surprised if, for most of you, there was. But I hope that has stimulated you to read on!

On the other hand, perhaps some of you reading the 'what mentors do not do' items above might now feel this book is not for you, especially if things written or said by people in your system seem to suggest that 'giving advice' or 'observing and giving feedback' are things you are required to do. The first thing is to question what any requirement actually is, and in most systems, as I have said, the main duty of a mentor is to support the mentee's learning (see Chapter 1). I believe the intention behind proposing or even requiring the activities of advice-giving and post-observation 'feedback' giving is benign and based on a belief that these are activities which support mentee learning. And they can – up to a point and with some mentees. However, while they may indeed support a type of contextual learning (how things are done here, what the expectations are for what good teaching should look like here), current research suggests they are also dangerous, limited, and a waste of time. They are dangerous because they support judgementoring with all its potentially negative outcomes (see above). They are limited because they do not support the learning of other crucial types of teacher knowledge (see below). They are likely to be a waste of time because they work with the judgementor's agenda, rather than with what the mentee is able to notice and is ready to learn. So, do read on. This book is for you too. It describes other activities that mentors do and can engage in which share the same aim of supporting mentee learning but which are less limited, less dangerous, and less wasteful of time. It also addresses the issue of your context and describes what other mentors have done when faced with seemingly being *required* to enact judgementoring practices.

You might like to return to these lists when you have read the whole book to see the sense you make of them then, whatever your first reactions to these lists.

Why the work of mentors is so important

In explanations of what I mean by certain key terms above (for example, 'effective' and 'mentoring'), I use the word 'learning.' What I mean by this also needs explanation. I hope briefly describing a way of seeing 'teacher learning' here will help me show you one reason why your work as a mentor is vital. I start with teacher knowledge. As teachers, we need to have and use three types of teacher knowledge. These categories group the 'what' is being learnt by 'how' it is learnt and correspond to the processes of learning required rather than what is learnt. Throughout our careers we need to and will need to:

1.   ***know about*** things (KA);
2.   ***know how*** to do things (KH); and
3.   ***know*** (intuitively or instinctively) ***to*** use that knowledge appropriately in class at just the right time to support our pupils' learning (KT).
     In addition, we need to combine these first three types of knowledge into an
4.   ***integrated knowledge-base*** (IKB) so that insights from our developing knowledge will emerge in our practice. We also need to develop the skills to continue to do this combining and integrating as we acquire new knowledge and have new experiences.

These different types of knowledge are not learnt in the same way nor under the same conditions. Some of this knowledge (KA and most of KH relating to classroom skills) can be and may best be learnt away from the school and the classroom. However, the type of intuitive knowledge that a teacher needs to use in order to make appropriate on the spot 'instinctive' decisions that help particular pupils continue their learning (KT) can *only* be learnt via and from experiences in schools and classrooms. Your role in this learning of KT is invaluable. So it is with IKB, a specific kind of KH learning. It is only in the process of planning, teaching, reviewing, and learning from actual teaching experiences that KA can be, as it were, folded into an integrated knowledge which makes a difference to what teachers actually do in classrooms. Being able to think about past experiences and plan for future experiences in classrooms (being able to think about and for experiences, in short) in a way which takes account of all types of knowledge is not a given. It requires learning. As with all kinds of learning of KH, this not only requires repeated practice but also can benefit from the support of a more-experienced 'other', and this is the second invaluable and irreplaceable role a mentor has in the process of teacher learning. I describe a way of working towards both KT and IKB later in the book which I have called Systematic Informed Reflective Practice (SIRP, Malderez, 2015). Chapter 6 lists further benefits of working in this way in post-lesson mentorials, but here I will mention just one more. Engaging in SIRP with the support of a mentor ensures the mentee develops what Claxton (2004) has termed "learnacy" or the ability to go on learning. It prepares the mentee with the skills and motivation to go on integrating new knowledge and new experiences into an ever-developing personal and practical knowledge base. It allows the development of teacher autonomy – the empowering 'E' of ONSIDE mentoring.

So, it is only mentors (in the sense I am meaning the term here) that can support the learning of two crucial types of teacher knowledge. I have used the words 'crucial' and 'vital' to describe your work because it is of little practical value if teachers know *about* things and can demonstrate that they *can* do things, if they don't actually use that knowledge and those skills in class when it matters. Nor is it enough to leave teachers in a state of learned helplessness, more or less dependent on the opinions and judgements of others, which judgementoring approaches encourage. Being in a state of learned helplessness is likely to result in less job satisfaction for the individual teacher, and this can lead to a higher risk of drop out. It is not wise from the point of view of the system either. Apart from the issue of retention, teachers deprived of opportunities to develop the skills associated with continued development and teacher autonomy are more likely to need resources (time, money, effort, more support) to adapt to the inevitable changes in the context over time, and they are less equipped to take account of insights from ongoing educational research.

I must briefly mention three further ways your work as a mentor helps your mentee and your education system, to try to show you just how important I think your work is.

1. For the last five decades at least, research has reported teachers as saying that they learn best from experience (see, e.g., Lortie, 1975; Hobson et al., 2009). Your role ensures they develop the skills and have the space to do this learning from experience, and that they learn not only from their own but from others' experience too.

2.   Before the advent of widespread mentoring, research reported the 'reality-shock' that beginning teachers experienced in their early years as a teacher in school which contributed to their choosing to drop out. More recent research (Malderez et al., 2007) conducted after the introduction of mentoring found that emotions still characterised the experience of those early years. Perhaps it is characteristic of any type of transformative learning (the type of learning which changes *you*, and what you actually do, not just what you say) at any stage of a teacher's career. Your Support role has a vital part to play in this regard.

3.   In our BaT research (Malderez et al., 2007; Hobson et al., 2009), we found four core themes which characterised the early experiences of people becoming teachers in England. We followed research participants from their last or only year on a programme leading to initial teaching qualifications through to the end of their fourth year in post. Apart from **emotions** (discussed above), research participants were preoccupied by **relationships** (with a range of people – from pupils, their parents, colleagues, tutors and their mentors), their **identity** (feeling like, looking like, being treated and trusted as a teacher) and the **relevance** of what they were being taught on their programme (KA and KH). Mentoring helps teachers address all of these themes. In particular, as part of the process of helping the mentee to review, analyse and learn from experiences (SIRP, see Chapter 6), your work supports the teacher in finding the practicality of 'theory' (KA) by discovering ways to *use* 'theory' in thinking and planning (for example, in explaining and understanding an occurrence in class or devising a solution to a problem). Our BaT study (cited above) found that, for many trainees, 'theory' seemed to mean *anything* others said which was not learnt through experiences in schools or classrooms. Even seemingly practical topics, such as writing lesson plans, were classed as 'theory.' SIRP helps address the immediate issue of **relevance** to student and early-career teachers of what they are studying elsewhere. Mentors don't have to know everything the mentee has learnt; they just have to help them remember and use what they have already been taught and perhaps introduce them to other ideas. I describe a way of doing that later in the book (Activity 1, in Chapter 6).

So much for mentees in the early years of their careers. But what about more-experienced teacher-mentees? As I said above, I think transformative learning involves emotions whenever it occurs, so your Support role is needed for all mentees. More-experienced teacher-mentees may have had the time to address the issues of identity and relationships initially, although they are likely to need revisiting from time to time, and it may be even more challenging for more-experienced teachers to contemplate adjusting these and become vulnerable again. As for the issue of **relevance**, I suspect that for some more-experienced teachers it still exists. I remember in my own early experiences as a teacher being told by an old hand to "forget all that theory, that waffle they taught you, I'll show you what we do here." Perhaps you are thinking, "That must have been ages ago. Surely things have changed?" That was indeed a while ago, but our BaT research has revealed that old hands are still saying similar things to student and early-career teachers. That's understandable – if they were never helped to see the practical use of 'theory' to them and their work and are in a system which does not in fact seem to value teacher autonomy (whatever the rhetoric).

So, your work is vital here too in helping mentees (and programmes leading to initial teaching qualifications or certification) close what we teachers of teachers (known variously as trainers, tutors or teacher educators, for example) call (called?) the theory-practice gap. When you, in your Model role, are engaged in your own SIRP and supporting your mentee through his or her SIRP in your Educator role, things can be different. Most of what mentees have been taught can become relevant, as long as the curriculum is thoughtful and designed based on what teachers need to know (rather than, for example, on the research interests of those who teach on the programme). In addition, if all teachers not only have access to but also a way of *using* relevant outcomes of new research, this can also help ensure the development of your education system as a whole in the longer term. (For an earlier version of most ideas in this section see Malderez, 2010.)

On the notion of 'help'

Mentoring is about helping mentees learn teaching. So, as well as understanding something about a learning teaching process, I needed to consider what *helping* someone through that process involves. If one of my sons, seeing me carrying lots of shopping bags, offers to help me, he is offering to carry them *for* me. However, as a mentor, my role is not to do things *for* the mentee but to help them do things for themselves.

The notion of scaffolding (Wood, Bruner and Ross, 1976) has been widely adopted as describing pedagogical help. It was one source which provided some guidance as to the *types of strategies* a mentor might employ and avoid the impulse to do things for the mentee – which might be much easier and quicker but is generally unhelpful in the pedagogical sense (but see Chapter 2). Scaffolding moves include:

- having the learner clarify what she/he wants to learn or do;
- breaking the process of doing 'it' into steps and prompting the learner from step to step ('it' in our mentoring context being any of the planning, teaching, reflecting and drawing conclusions and making judgements, decisions and new plans, as well as the teaching itself);

- providing clues, prompts or explanations only in response to evidence that, without them, the learner's progress is stalled;
- ensuring that it is the learner who 'does it', and not 'doing it for them'; and
- ensuring the learner recognises his or her own achievements and progress.

Together with the view of teacher knowledge and the contexts and processes which support its learning, this notion of scaffolding was very important in the development of the approach described in this book and particularly in the various mentorial protocols described in Chapter 6.

Comparing mentoring with other Teachers of Teachers (ToTs)

One final way of defining something is to compare it with other similar things. So here, using ideas presented above, I have compared teacher mentoring in Table 0.1 with other types of ToTs.

Table 0.1 Features in the work of various types of ToTs

Feature or Focus>	Works 1 to 1	Works 1 to Group	Scaffolds	KA	KH	KT	IKB	Assesses
ToT Type								
Mentor	X		X	(x)	(x)	X	X	
Trainer	X	X	(x)		X			X
Lecturer		X	(x)	X	(x)			X

Notes on Table 0.1

- ToT = Teacher of Teachers. This is a broad 'umbrella' term for anyone whose task it is to support teacher learning.

- Large X = the main feature; Small (x) in parentheses = usually not the main feature although there may be opportunities on occasion, depending on the mode of working and perhaps the size of the group. For example, a trainer, whose main focus is on developing KH, is able to scaffold in one-to-one training situations, but will be less able to do so when working with groups. Scaffolding is only consistently possible in one-to-one situations. So, a mentor, because by definition she/he works one to one, is always in a position to scaffold her or his mentee's learning, making every intervention contingent on the particular mentee's reactions, actions and emotions.

There is one other comparison, I think, that is worth making here too – that between teacher mentoring and coaching, described in Table 0.2, and discussed below.

Table 0.2 Mentors and coaches compared

Roles and Focus	Support	Acculturator	Model	Sponsor	Educator: Reflective Practice	Educator: Teacher Learning	Works with other professions
Mentors	X	X	X	X	X	X	
Coaches	(x)				X		X

Despite the recommendation of Hobson = van Nieuwerburgh (2022) that both coaches and mentors working with teachers should read each other's literature, I can't claim to have done so in equal measure. In some coaching literature, I have found characterisations of 'mentoring' when being compared to coaching to be very far from my view presented in this book, so I hope I have not made a similar mistake with my understanding of coaching! My view of coaching stems from discussions with coaches as well as fairly limited recent reading. In addition, unlike the ToT types in Table 0.1, I have no personal experience of being a coach. I do have a *very* limited experience of being coached by someone called a 'life coach' decades ago, if that counts. Earlier in this chapter I quoted Elaine Cox's definition of coaching as being "facilitated reflective practice." Mentors, too, facilitate reflective practice by guiding mentees through the SIRP process (see Chapter 6). In facilitating reflective practice, neither coaches nor mentors judge or advise (which can also come from a place of judgement) or make decisions or plans *for* the people they work with. Both work one to one towards the growth and development of those they work with and aim towards real-world actions and impact. Both take their lead from the person they work with. Both listen more than they talk in their formal sessions or mentorials. This explains why I have included a small (x) under Support for coaches. Being actively listened to during facilitated reflective practice can be cathartic and supportive, too, even if it was not the main purpose of the listening. (Incidentally, research interviews can fulfil a similar by-product function too. The participants in the case study strand of our BaT project said how much they had looked forward to the annual interview, over five years. They valued the opportunity to think back over their year and to talk and be listened to.)

That is where I see the similarities and overlaps ending. The SIRP protocol (Chapter 6) has another vital function which was the main one in my mind as I developed it. This has to do with teacher learning and learnacy development, and the steps of the protocol are the scaffolding steps of that particular professional learning process and address the particular needs and challenges of the teaching profession. Mentors have many other research-informed roles to enact, too; coaches don't, as far as I understand it. Teacher mentors need to be teachers themselves, coaches don't. Coaches are not teacher mentors, although teacher mentors may be said to be coaching in one specific part of one of their five roles. Coaches work with a wide range of people in various contexts and for various purposes. Teacher mentors work only with teachers for the purposes of supporting their mentees' learning from their own and others' experiences in ways which positively affect future experiences of teaching and pupil learning, and specifically:

- to close 'theory-practice' gaps and contribute to the development of the profession;
- for the development of their KT (via noticing development, see SIRP step 1); and

- for the development of IKB (via reflective practice that is facilitated, repeated, systematic, and, specifically, *informed*).

In addition, a mentor's work in their non-educator roles helps ensure optimal conditions for such professional learning and integration to take place.

It occurs to me, writing this, that perhaps the proliferation of judgementoring – understood as mentoring – and dissatisfaction with it, might explain why some have turned to coaching. It might explain the addition of 'and coaching' to the term 'mentoring' in the current use of the phrase 'mentoring and coaching' for teachers in places such as England. I hope this book can contribute to restoring the reputation of mentoring.

A few words about language

I have already mentioned my disquiet at some of the common terms used in education today. I could attribute my dislike to such things as the 'marketisation' or 'businessification' of education, but from my perspective as a teacher and mentor, a practitioner, it is mainly because they are misleading and/or unhelpful. Learning, as we have seen, cannot be reduced to (only) the 'delivery' or handing over of knowledge (usually understood as KA knowledge). So for me, the metaphor of 'delivery' to describe what teachers do is at best unhelpful and at worst dangerous: dangerous because metaphors are powerful tools in transformative teacher learning (see Chapter 8, 'Modes of mind'). The use of 'delivery' reinforces an outdated view of a teacher as a 'teller.' I will be explaining my dislike of a number of other expressions which I think are unhelpful to you and your mentee throughout the book. For example, in the next chapter, I go back to my problems with the expressions 'give or provide (constructive) feedback' and 'best practice', and in Conclusions, I question the term 'adaptive teaching' in more detail.

"Words don't have meanings, *people* have meanings they use words to express." I forget where I first read or heard that, as it was back in the days when I was a language teacher, and at the time I did not intend to cite it in writing, just use it in my thinking. I do try to be very careful that the words I use will express my meanings to you. This is perhaps easier to do in writing than in speaking, even if writing, to me as a teacher, has always been a painful exercise. I can and do ask friends and colleagues to give me readers' responses to drafts (see Acknowledgements) and go back and edit. On the other hand, I don't personally know each 'you' that is reading these words or how you might interpret them. When I speak to someone, I have the advantage of being able to notice how my words are received, and I try again if I feel I haven't got my meanings across. I don't, though, have the advantage of being able to edit out or take back my words when speaking. So, for this reason, as well as trying to avoid misleading or unhelpful language, I found as a mentor I needed to be very careful of the words I used with my mentees. I learnt, for example, to (try to) avoid 'advice-giving' (judgementoring) language in most roles. For example, I avoided 'you should', replacing it with 'you could' – but then only if absolutely necessary. Mentees are usually expert at 'listening between the lines', and depending on your relationship, they may perceive what you genuinely meant only as a suggestion as an order or prescription! Groups of mentors I have worked with have developed lists of 'Mentor Taboo Words' and 'should' is usually one of the first words on these. If you are working through this book with one or more colleagues and role-playing some of the processes and activities described (see 'How you might want to use this book' below), you might like to (or 'you could') develop your own 'Taboo Words' list as a result of the experiences. If you are a practising mentor, you might like to record a mentorial (with your mentee's permission) in order to consider your actual use of language and choice of words and any evidence of impact – especially unintended impact (and see Chapter 8). This would have the additional advantage of making your work on your own development as a mentor more visible to your mentee and help you fulfil your Model role (see Chapter 4).

There are, therefore, two main reasons why, in descriptions of some processes in this book, I have written some of the actual words mentors use. The first is that our use of language can betray our judgements of our mentee's work if we are not very careful and can make us seem a bit of a judgementor.' (We inevitably *have* judgements that ideally we only use to help us decide what we need to do next with and for our mentees.) In fact, we will speak as we were spoken to unless we are very careful. Unless we are lucky enough to have had a mentor ourselves, our instinctive way of talking – especially in the Educator role when 'safe' non-judgemental language is most needed – is unlikely to be that of a mentor.

By now some of you may be wondering about such things as:

- how do we build trusting relationships without meaningful (personal, potentially hurtful) sharing (see Chapters 2 and 7); and
- don't our mentees expect to hear judgements? (it's only human!) (see Chapters 6 and 7)

These are actual examples of what I call 'yes, buts', the reservations mentors I have worked with, or who have been kind enough to read drafts of this book, have had when coming to grips with this approach. These and other 'yes, buts' will be addressed in more detail as the book progresses. For now, can I simply say that my responses relate to starting the relationship, being clear what role you are in, and stages of teacher development, and suggest you read on?

In summary, my first reason for showing 'safe' mentoring language and ways of talking is that I hope it may be helpful to you. The second is to do with my efforts at trying to help you visualise what effective mentoring might look like.

Of course, you may not be mentoring in English. Even if you are both teachers of English as a foreign or second language, it may be more comfortable and natural to conduct your relationship in a shared, familiar, local language. It may also be better, in the Educator role at least, even though you are both missing the opportunity to hone your English-speaking skills. I say that because many of the ideas you will be considering and discussing are complex and because knowledge of and skills in the subject your mentee is teaching are only two small parts of what he or she is learning. Another reason for not using English in these contexts might be if your fluency in English is considerably greater than that of your mentee. This might jeopardise the perception of a non-hierarchical relationship and make achieving ONSIDE mentoring more challenging. But contexts are different, including each mentor–mentee relationship (see Chapter 2). You may want to add a discussion on 'what language to use when' on your 'to do' list for your initial, agreement-making meeting with your mentee (see Chapter 2). If you are not using English for some or all of your mentor roles, you will need, ideally before you start mentoring, to think about commonly used individual words, expressions and bits of educational jargon in your language that might be unhelpful in mentoring and consider alternatives.

What is in the book

What follows are brief summaries of what is in each chapter.

Chapter 1 How far does your context support mentoring?

This initial chapter proposes that you might usefully undertake, even before the mentoring relationship begins, a 'contextual mentoring audit' in order to identify those aspects of your own context (at the levels of the relationship, school, the region and the system) which might affect the effectiveness of your work or your mentee's learning. Questions to guide your investigations are proposed. Once done, you can devise strategies, and/or select from those used by other mentors, to 'protect' your mentee from the more negative aspects in your context (and so remain ONSIDE) and to take advantage of the positive ones.

Chapter 2 Mentor Role 1: Support – supporting your mentee as a person

This chapter highlights the importance of the Support role in the process of mentoring. It addresses the issues of trust and how to be trustworthy and interpersonal relationships and how to start and maintain them, recognising a mentee's emotional states and ways of adjusting mentoring practice accordingly. The second section discusses the vital mentor skill of active listening. Finally, the chapter briefly discusses times when doing things 'for' the mentee might occasionally be appropriate (in contrast with the Educator role) in order to be supportive of the person.

Chapter 3 Mentor Role 2: Acculturator - helping your mentee adjust to the school and the profession

This chapter considers the Acculturator role in the 'five mentor roles' model the book proposes. Strategies others use to support the mentee in gaining full membership of the cultures of the school and the wider profession are listed. I also discuss what the role requires of you as a person and as a professional (for example, that you would ideally already be a full member of all the various professional communities at whatever level of context that you are helping your mentee join).

Chapter 4 Mentor Role 3: Model - modelling professionalism

As we cannot claim that there is one 'right' way of teaching, rarely will a mentor need or want to model (any aspect of) 'how to teach.' Occasions when this might, however, be appropriate are listed. Rather, a mentor's main duty in this Model role is to model how to *be* a professional teacher. The various aspects of what it means to be a professional are outlined, and the challenges of this role are discussed. For example, some vital aspects of professionalism are usually invisible. As always, practical ways others have tried to overcome these challenges are listed.

Chapter 5 Mentor Role 4: Sponsor - using your knowledge and contacts to help your mentee

In this chapter, I turn to the Sponsor role. The chapter provides specific examples of how this role could be, and has been, enacted. In the model of mentoring this book proposes, our duty is not to produce clones of ourselves, but rather to support our mentees in developing their own teaching style and identity. So, the need for you to talk about your own practice as a teacher, what you do and why, is less than in some models. This issue is, however, addressed in this chapter, under the various types of knowledge a mentor might have and be able to share with their mentee. Times when it might be appropriate to share this type of knowledge (and when not) are also discussed.

Chapter 6 Mentor Role 5: Educator - helping the mentee learn and learn to learn teaching

If the previous roles are about a mentor's personal support for their mentee and ways to help the mentee become, be and remain a teacher, this chapter is all about the mentee's classroom teaching and learning (of all types of knowledge, but particularly of KT and IKB).

Included in this core chapter are protocols for post-lesson mentorials (SIRP) and for pre-lesson mentorials. I give reasons for the form and use of such activities, including a section on noticing. I provide a format for a Mentorial Record Sheet and a section on providing other learning opportunities (for example, facilitating the mentee's access to the classes of colleagues who are expert in the aspect of teaching that the mentee is working on).

Chapter 7 Dealing with assessing your mentees (and with others' assessments of them)

This chapter is particularly for those readers unlucky enough to be required by their system to also 'assess' their mentee and report their judgements to the mentee and others. I write 'unlucky enough' because, amongst other negative effects, this requirement puts the safe trusting relationship which is fundamental to effective mentoring at risk. It makes the mentor's crucial role much more difficult in many ways. However, in the cases where, as things stand, these duties cannot be given to others (so that the mentor can remain on the side of the mentee and can work with the mentee on any results of any outsider's assessments), ways others have attempted to accomplish this combining of conflicting duties with the minimum amount of disruption to an effective mentoring process are described.

Chapter 8 Developing as a mentor

As part of your 'model' role, you will want to be engaged in your own ongoing learning of teaching and will need to find ways to make this visible to your mentee. You will also want and need to learn from your experiences of mentoring. Ways others have used to do this are described, including activities to use alone in addition to SIRP and for use in groups of mentors. The second half of the chapter includes a 'starter set' of ideas from others that might be useful in step 3 of your systematic, informed reflections on your mentoring processes.

Chapter 9 Stories

In this chapter, you will find three of the allegorical stories which mentors have found useful to experience and which have contributed to their development (see 'Why I have written this book', above). I invite you to ponder how each story relates to your mentoring and the messages you can take. I provide a brief description of how I prepare to tell such stories (in case you might want to tell one in a mentor meeting). My commentaries, and the messages other mentors have taken from each story, can be found at the end of the chapter.

Chapter 10 Conclusions

In this final chapter, I highlight some of the ideas presented in the book as they might be relevant to various types of reader. I include three professional stories to illustrate the benefits to you that becoming, being and developing as a mentor can bring. Finally, I look to the future of mentoring as a feature of education systems and as a profession.

How you could use the book

As a writer, I am thinking of you starting with this introduction and reading through to the end. At some point, at least, I hope you will find the time to do this. In other words, the book is not initially structured for a dipping-in approach. Having said that, I am realistic. I hope I have made the contents of each chapter sufficiently clear above so that, when you are faced with a specific dilemma or query, or when you are working on a specific aspect of your mentoring practice, you can locate the relevant chapter. For this reason, when a particular idea or practice builds or depends on ideas presented elsewhere in the book, these are signposted.

The stories in Chapter 9 could also be used as 'respite reading' by those of you reading from cover to cover. By 'respite reading', I mean that if the reading gets tough for you, or you feel you have more than enough to digest and you need a break, you could read one of the stories in Chapter 9 before putting the book down. (Read Stories 1 and 2 at any time, but save Story 3 until after Chapter 6!)

Working with others

You might be in a position where you are going to, or can arrange opportunities to, discuss ideas in this book with fellow mentors. In which case, you could do more than simply discuss and, for example:

- work on developing listening skills together (see Chapters 2 and 8);
- role-play or practise using some of the practical ideas (particularly mentorial protocols in Chapter 6);
- arrange meetings of mentors to sustain ongoing development (see Chapter 8); or
- rehearse storytelling (Chapter 9).

The next chapter contains a number of questions to ask yourselves and find answers to about your context. As I believe it is preferable to have undertaken this task before you start your mentoring, it comes first in the main chapters. However, if you are pushed for time or want to get to the meat of the description of mentoring as enacted in this approach, you could turn to Chapters 2 to 6 first and return to Chapter 1 after this.

References

Claxton, G. (2004), Learning is learnable (and we ought to teach it). In J. Cassell (Ed.) *Ten years on*. Bristol: National Commission for Education.

Cox, E. (2012), *Coaching understood: a pragmatic inquiry into the coaching process*. London: Sage.

Hobson, A.J. (2016), Judgementoring and how to avert it: introducing ONSIDE mentoring for beginning teachers. *International Journal of Mentoring and Coaching in Education*, Vol. 5, No. 2, pp. 87-110.

Hobson, A.J., Asby, P., Malderez, A. & Tomlinson, P.D. (January 2009), Mentoring beginning teachers: what we know and what we don't. *Teaching and Teacher Education*, Vol. 25, No. 1, pp. 207-216.

Hobson, A.J. & Malderez, A. (2013), Judgementoring and other threats to realizing the potential of school-based mentoring in teacher education. *International Journal of Mentoring and Coaching in Education*, Vol. 2, No. 2, pp. 89-108.

Hobson, A.J., Malderez, A., Tracey, L., Homer, M.S., Ashby, P. & Mitchell, N. (2009), *Becoming a teacher: teachers' experiences of initial teacher training, induction and early professional development. Final report*. DCSF Research Report DCSF-RR115. London: Department of Education and Skills.

Hobson, A.J. = van Nieuwerburgh, C.J. (2022), Extending the research agenda on (ethical) coaching and mentoring in education: embracing mutuality and prioritising well-being. *International Journal of Mentoring and Coaching in Education*, Vol. 11, No. 1, pp. 1-13.

Lortie, D. (1975), *School teacher: a sociological study*. Chicago: University of Chicago Press.

Malderez, A. (2004), A teacher educator's story of developing understanding. In D. Hayes (Ed.) *Trainer development: principles and practice from language teacher training*. Melbourne: Language Australia, pp. 21-50.

Malderez, A. (2010), A case for mentoring: why (beginning) teachers (and education systems) need mentors. In J.-C. Loos et al (Eds.) *L'accompagnement des nouveaux enseignants*. Bruxelles: EME, pp. 51-62.

Malderez, A. (2015), Mentoring in supporting (English) teacher learning: where are we now? In D. Holló & K. Károly (Eds.) *Inspirations in foreign language teaching – studies in language pedagogy and applied linguistics*. Harlow: Pearson Education, pp. 21-32.

Malderez, A. & Bodòczky, C. (1999), *Mentor courses: a resource book for trainer trainers*. Cambridge: Cambridge University Press.

Malderez, A., Hobson, A.J., Tracey, L. & Kerr, K. (2007), Becoming a student teacher: core features of the experience. *European Journal of Teacher Education*, Vol. 30, No. 3, pp. 225-248.

Malderez, A. & Wedell, M. (2007), *Teaching teachers: processes and practices*. London: Continuum.

Wood, D., Bruner, J.S. & Ross, G. (1976), The role of tutoring in problem-solving. *Journal of Child Psychology and Psychiatry*, Vol. 17, pp. 89-100.

1 How far does your context support mentoring?

A pre-mentoring task

Introduction

This chapter proposes a thinking task so you can have a closer look at your context and determine how far it is likely to be supportive of your work. This task, this 'contextual mentoring audit' (CMA), is one that mentors, as well as those developing and/or leading mentoring schemes, might usefully undertake even before any mentoring begins. As you respond to the questions posed in this short chapter, you should be able to identify those aspects of your own context which might affect the effectiveness of your work and the extent of your mentee's learning. Once you have thought about your context in this way, you can devise strategies, and/or select from those used by other mentors given in the examples below, which might help you 'protect' your mentee from the more negative aspects and so remain 'ONSIDE' (Hobson, 2016, see Introduction) or take advantage of the positive ones.

No two contexts are the same, and what your context is like can make a difference in how successful your mentoring is. You know your context, you are familiar with it, and can probably already spot aspects which might or might not be helpful. So why am I writing this chapter? There are three main reasons. The first has to do with that very familiarity. When we are familiar with something (or somewhere or someone), we stop consciously noticing it or aspects of it (see Chapter 6, On Noticing). It becomes taken for granted, and we can fail to realise its potential impact which can jeopardise our mentoring before it begins. The second is to emphasise again (Wedell and Malderez, 2013) how important context is in any educational endeavour. My final reason for including this chapter is to share some strategies mentors have used as a result of undertaking a closer look at their own context.

I have used the word 'context' many times above and want now to provide a brief explanation of what I mean by this term, so that the various headings and questions in the CMA below will make more sense when you encounter them. Martin Wedell and I proposed a detailed way of thinking about 'context' in our 2013 book (see References), but here is a simple summary. Context is about

DOI: 10.4324/9781003429005-2

place at various levels, such as country, school, classroom. It is also about the *people* who are in and creating the cultures of those places as well as the particular groupings of people: peoples' biographies and interactions matter. Thirdly, 'context' encompasses the notion of *time*. For example, it will make a difference when in the lives or professional biographies of the people in your context (or when in the broader history of time) you undertake your audit. Finally, doing an audit can be complicated by the fact that any context, or any aspect of it, has both visible and invisible sides: you can notice what a staffroom looks and feels like, but you can't easily see the thinking, beliefs and cultural norms behind the decisions that led to it being like that.

Throughout this chapter, I have used some examples drawn from one context: England. Although almost all of the practical experience I have of mentoring is from elsewhere in the world, I returned to live in England and have conducted research here. (See Hobson et al., 2009; Hobson, Malderez and Tracey, 2009). These examples are included as just that, examples. There are huge differences in teacher preparation programmes around the world in terms of length, format, content and site. These may last from one to five years and differ in whether or not they:

- include and embed work on the subject specialism to be taught;
- are about more than KA knowledge acquisition, or more than localised KH acquisition;
- include a formal school-based mentored strand of work within the programme, or
- take place in an HE provider or a school.

Increasingly, it seems to me, England is moving Initial Teacher Preparation into schools, causing the ToTs to make considerable adjustments (see Brown et al., 2015). In other places, people are now adding both KH knowledge development and a mentored school-based element into their HE programmes.

Contextual mentoring audit

You will probably be able to think of responses to most of the following questions as you read them. Some may require some investigation on your part. When you have a response, read or re-read the commentary and strategies sections which follow each group of questions. You might then want to make yourself a 'to do' list, as necessary, and endeavour to take those actions before you begin the mentoring process.

The questions here are not exhaustive, and it is likely that you will think of more, prompted perhaps by the categories. It may be helpful to undertake this exercise with other mentors in your local context.

International context

Mentoring

Which international journals and conferences address or include mentoring for teachers and teaching?

Teaching

Which are the main journals and conferences for teachers of your discipline?

Country

Mentoring

- Is mentoring teachers common in your country?

If so,

- What is meant by mentoring?
- How and when is it used?
- Who are the mentees?
- Are there any government documents about mentoring teachers?
- Are there any explicit published standards for mentors? (see example below in my Reflections section)
- How, if at all, are mentors valued and recognised?
- Do mentors of teachers have their own professional body, journals and conferences? If not, are they explicitly included in other professional groupings?

Teaching

- Are there general Teaching Standards published in your context? (e.g., from England, see DfE 2011)
- Are there explicit published standards for teachers of your discipline? How are these ensured or assessed?
- Do teachers of your (and your mentee's) discipline have their own professional body, journals and conferences at the national level?

———————

Commentary

Discovering available resources such as journals, documents or relevant conferences will probably be a long-term project and may not be possible to complete before you start mentoring. The references sections of this book could be one small starting point.

Understanding contextual meanings of the term 'mentoring' is also probably a longer-term project. To my knowledge, the term 'mentoring' has been used in connection with supporting teacher learning, at least in some parts of the world, since the 1980s. Mentoring for business/career development/managerial purposes is much older. It might be helpful to determine whether definitions you find, or practices you know about, seem to belong to one of either 'mentoring for teacher learning' or 'mentoring for career development.' Then ask yourself whether models that ostensibly fall under the 'teacher learning' category might more accurately be described as 'mentoring' (for KT and IKB development) or as 'one-to-one training for initial teacher training' (for developing KH where there is one right or expected method or way of teaching – a 'best practice'). Indeed, are they in fact more about 'assessment' than supporting learning and wellbeing? This fairly long history of supporting professionals via a one-to-one relationship has several major implications for new mentoring projects, depending on where you are in the world. Firstly, 40 years of mentoring in teacher education have led to a plethora of meanings for the term. In some places (particularly Europe), the practices of coaching are used in lieu of or in addition to mentoring in the supported development of professionals, including teachers. In England, for example, national publications refer to 'mentoring *and* coaching', whereas for me, a type of coaching could be said to be a *part* of mentoring (see Introduction). So being clear, very clear, on what you want to mean by it, as well as how your meaning differs, if at all, from any published national definitions, will be crucial. Secondly, as teachers-becoming-mentors, you may or may not have had experience yourself of being 'mentored.' This may or may not be helpful to you now. When I have asked those teachers-becoming-mentors who have had the experience of being mentored what their mentors did with or for them, most have mentioned practices I would associate with either training or assessment. Therefore, it may be no surprise when I say I have found it comparatively much easier to work with teachers-becoming-mentors in contexts where teacher mentoring was a relatively new concept and participants arrived with no experiential knowledge of working with someone called a mentor.

Considering how and when something viewed as teacher mentoring is or has been used in your context will be similarly important too. In some contexts, understood in its broad sense, for example, mentoring is or has been compulsory for both participants or even seen as a 'fix' for failing teachers (see Conclusions). These are considerations mainly for the mentoring co-ordinator when developing the aims of the mentoring programme you are or will be part of, but it may also affect aspects of your work too. It's no fun trying to be a mentor to a reluctant or resentful mentee!

In one context I have worked in where participation was compulsory, mentors had to focus hard initially on the vital Support role and the most immediate aspect of context: the mentor-mentee relationship (see Chapter 2).

In another context I have worked in, where mentoring had been used to try to 'fix' failing teachers, early-/mid-career teachers were reluctant to volunteer to participate in a new mentoring scheme as mentoring had become associated in their minds as a strategy only for 'bad teachers' and they didn't want to be seen as such. Some of the new mentors therefore chose to volunteer as mentees in the early stages of the project, until the word spread and the 'buzz' in the staffroom encouraged others to volunteer eventually. An added benefit was that the mentors who had first been mentees began their mentoring with enriched understandings.

Increasingly mentor standards for teacher professional development are being or have been drafted. You may find some for your context. Most I have seen use words like 'constructive criticism' and/or mention 'observation', both of which I associate with judgementoring or training (see Introduction). However, all seem to see mentoring as a strategy to support teacher learning. Mentors I have worked with have therefore chosen to respond to the teacher learning/ development aims (rather than any standards couched in judgementoring or training terms) and focus on all five roles. In the Educator role, they focused on the development of their mentee's noticing for KT development and in their abilities to form an integrated and informed teacher knowledge via a process of scaffolded professional learning from their own and others' experiences (such as SIRP, see Chapter 6). Where observations and provision of 'feedback' are both required and inescapable, these practices can be used for training discrete aspects of teaching which the mentee has identified as one of their learning goals, and 'trainer' activities are added to those of a mentor. Ideas for how to also add assessor duties can be found in Chapter 7.

Searching for up-to-date documents here in England to provide examples for this book, the only published 'mentor standards' I initially found (DfE 2016) were those associated with the school-based mentoring of student teachers in partnership with programmes preparing them for qualifications and Qualified Teacher Status (Initial Teacher Training, ITT). These are non-statutory standards (rather than being legal requirements) and are for guidance only. I'm glad. Overall, I find the categories confusing both in their content and in the choice of number of standards as well as the headings. For example, as these are standards for mentors and their mentoring, why is there one headed "teaching"? Why is the item "resolve in-school issues on the trainee's behalf where they lack the confidence or experience to do so themselves" – which I can see as a possible activity in a Sponsor role – under the heading 'teaching'?

I made three pages of notes and queries! I'm going to give you some extracts from my notes here as an example of the kind of careful scrutiny you will need to do on any 'Mentor Standards' you find. My starting point was to pick out various key phrases (see 'A few words about language' in the Introduction) used under the four standards proposed.

Standard 1 Personal qualities

"Use appropriate challenge to encourage the trainee to reflect on their practice."

I'm not sure how this is a 'personal quality' of a mentor. It is not something any teacher brings with them to the role. Supporting someone to learn the skills and willingness to engage in meaningful informed reflection requires skills that need time to develop - and the starting point is not a mentor's "challenge", but rather something the mentee noticed in their class.

Standard 2 Teaching

"Give constructive, clear and timely feedback on lesson observations."

See comments on the use and meanings of the term 'feedback' in Chapter 6. For now, I'll just say that this would seem to be ideal conditions for judgementoring to occur if the full lesson is in focus. Otherwise, they - observations and feedback - could be used for training a particular teaching skill, which is not as a rule, even with pre-qualification mentees, a mentor's role, although supporting a mentee in recalling their training and honing those skills will be.

The rest of this standard lists things the mentor should ensure the student teacher learns.

"Best practice"

What do observers want to see? 'Best practice' for whom, where, when? Is there really anything we could call 'best practice'? Good, useful, perhaps. But *the* best, singular? Does this mean an item on the student-teacher's curriculum for KH development that they are expected to learn? If so, this is for training.

Standard 3 Professionalism

When I first read the title of this standard, I was expecting something about reflective practice and developing the abilities to make their own informed decisions. However, the only possible connection with my understanding of the term is a reference to personal and professional conduct (see Chapter 4). Other parts seem more related to the Acculturator role or aspects of the trainee's curriculum.

Standard 4 Self-development and partnership

"Moderate [verb] judgements"

If mentors are involved in assessments, it will be a real challenge (see Chapter 7) for them to also be non-evaluative (the 'N' of ONSIDE).

I would label these standards as for 'one-to-one training' and 'assessing' rather than mentoring. The full document, which includes the details of the standards, provides case studies which describe observations and the provision of "constructive feedback." These are needed when training particular predetermined skills for teaching, or a particular piece of KH. KH development can, and in my view should, be trained before a student teacher arrives in a classroom. Also, elsewhere in the document, it is seen as a good thing that mentors are also senior leaders (not what Hobson's review of recent research suggests – the 'O' of ONSIDE being 'offline', see Introduction). So for me, these standards would only be more or less appropriate in contexts where teaching skills development, possibly through observations of teaching followed by repeated micro-teaching practice, has not occurred before and if there is no additional mentoring of the kind I describe this book, where the aim is simply to try to replicate existing practices, where the programme does not aim to produce reflective practitioners and professionals and where there is no expectation that educational research related to teaching will ever have an impact on future teaching.

More recently, the guidelines (rather than standards) for Mentors of Early Career Teachers (first two years in post after qualification) elicited very few notes from me (DfE 2022).

As a final word on standards, I have drafted some core mentor standards to which further standards may be added according to context, ones appropriate for additional Trainer or assessor duties, for example. My core mentor standards are in the appendix of this book, as they will make more sense when you have read on. However, unlike everything else I describe which has been developed and trialled in many contexts over years, these are new and written specifically for this book.

Region

Ask yourself the same questions as for 'Country' above (substituting 'regional' for 'national'). If there are differences between your answers at different levels, why might this be?

School/Institution

Mentoring

- Does formal mentoring already occur across your institution or school, or in other subjects, disciplines or departments?

If so,

- What type of mentoring is it? (mentoring-for-career-development or mentoring-to-support-teachers'-professional-development')
- What do these mentors actually do?
- Does it follow ONSIDE (see Introduction) principles in its organisation?
- How are mentors prepared to begin mentoring?
- Is mentor development supported?
- What kind of formal recognition for mentors, if any, is accorded?

Teaching

- How often does any formal quality assurance of teaching occur?
- Who undertakes this?
- Does this make explicit use of any published national standards?
- Are published discipline/subject-specific interpretations of broad standards for teaching also in use?
- What types of formal support for the professional development of teachers and teaching already exist?
- Do colleagues feel any formal group support for development is relevant to them and time well spent?
- Do interactions about teaching between colleagues occur spontaneously? When, where and why?

Commentary

Looking again at your immediate context will not only ensure you are equipped with knowledge you may need in carrying out various roles, but it might also alert you to actions you might like to take before the mentoring begins. For example, research has shown (Hobson et al., 2009) that an important characteristic of a mentor for mentees is their 'availability.' This can be seen in two ways: proximity and time. Thinking about the former, a mentor decided to ensure her mentee was in the same staffroom. Later, when her mentee came in after a lesson looking pretty downcast, she reported that she was able in a Support role (and while quickly passing to go to a lesson of her own) to sympathise and empathise while suggesting that the lesson could be the one they worked on in their next mentorial. She said something like, "Oh, I hope my lesson doesn't make me feel like you seem to be feeling.... All of us have lessons like that sometimes.... We can talk about it at our next mentorial perhaps?" Our mentee's feelings or impulsive judgements – whether positive or negative – are big clues of where a readiness-to-learn might be. (See Chapter 6.) The time aspect of availability will largely have been decided by the programme designer or coordinator. But, as the example above shows, 'being there' for your mentee need not take huge amounts of extra time. However, you may want to discuss this aspect of availability with other mentors in your context. For example, some mentors have given mentees their phone numbers, while others have not; some have limited this availability to working hours, but some have not. Finding and agreeing to boundaries of availability will be a necessary part of an initial mentee-mentor meeting (see Chapter 2), and so it will be important to discuss and agree to these boundaries beforehand.

Other research has shown (Elmajdob, 2004) that if there are any members of staff in your context who, in their interactions with your mentee, act as "alienators", "stressors", "restrictors" or "disempowerers", it will hamper your mentee's learning. You probably know already who those people might be. Is there anything you can do beforehand to 'protect' your mentee? Some mentor coordinators have held staff meetings before the mentoring begins at which they explain a bit about the scheme and can ask for everyone's cooperation (easier in a staffroom where cooperation rather than competition is the norm). Ensuring your mentee is in the same staffroom as you, apart from dealing with the proximity issue, can take the mentee out of the immediate orbit of likely alienators or stressors, or at the very least allow you to spot those negative interactions taking place and either jump in to protect your mentee ("sorry to interrupt, we have a meeting now") or have a quiet word later with the alienator/stressor.

So, having read this chapter, you probably have a to do list now. Try to accomplish those related to your local context before you begin mentoring, but don't worry if some of the more distant contextual questions take longer – much longer. If you are lucky, the mentor coordinator of your scheme will have taken issues discussed here into consideration. If not, she/he may be your first stop.

Perhaps the most important aspect of the context is your relationship with your mentee, and this is a main topic in the next chapter on your Support role.

References

Brown, T., Rowley, H. & Smith, K. (2015), Sliding subject positions: knowledge and teacher educators. *British Educational Research Journal*, Vol. 42, No. 3, pp. 492–507.

DfE. (2011), *Teachers' standards*. DfE, updated 2021. Accessed January 2023 at: www.gov.uk/government/publications/teachers-standards

DfE. (2016), *National standards for school-based initial teacher training ITT mentors*. DfE. Accessed April 2022 at: https://docplayer.net/22636146-National-standards-for-school-based-initial-teacher-training-itt-mentors.html

DfE. (2022), *Guidance for mentors: how to support ECF-based training*. DfE. Accessed February 2023 at: www.gov.uk/guidance/guidance-for-mentors-how-to-support-ecf-based-training

Elmajdob, A.H. (2004), *The roles played by relationships of Arab expatriate teachers in Libya: a case study*. PhD thesis. Leeds: University of Leeds.

Hobson, A.J. (2016), Judgementoring and how to avert it: introducing ONSIDE mentoring for beginning teachers. *International Journal of Mentoring and Coaching in Education*, Vol. 5, No. 2, pp. 87–110.

Hobson, A.J., Malderez, A. & Tracey, L. (2009), *Navigating initial teacher training: becoming a teacher*. London: Routledge.

Hobson, A.J., Malderez, A., Tracey, L., Homer, M.S., Ashby, P. & Mitchell, N. (2009), *Becoming a teacher: teachers' experiences of initial teacher training, induction and early professional development. Final report*. DCSF Research Report DCSF-RR115. London: Department of Education and Skills.

Wedell, M. & Malderez, A. (2013), *Understanding language classroom contexts: the starting point for change*. London: Bloomsbury.

2 Mentor Role 1: Support

Supporting your mentee as a person

Your relationship with your mentee is the closest and arguably most important aspect of the particular context for learning (see Chapter 1) that you find yourselves in. It is also the one you can have the most influence on as you are its co-creator.

This chapter begins therefore with ideas for starting, maintaining and ending your relationship with your mentee so that it is supportive of teacher learning. Ideally, your relationship will be one which is confidential and has, at its heart, trust and understanding. I like that last word – understanding – as it reminds us of the need to 'stand under' another, to see the world from another's perspective. I am reminded, too, of a favourite quote from Guy Claxton which uses the metaphors of a journey for learning and of placing stepping stones for teaching: "you can't put down stepping stones for someone to find without first knowing where they are" (Claxton, 1997). For me, "knowing where they are" is not only about knowing the stage our mentees have reached on their learning teaching journeys but also about knowing them as people. The more we understand about our mentee's prior experiences, background, fears, hopes, preferences and so on, the more accurately we can choose and place those stepping stones, that is, scaffold (see Introduction) their learning.

Our BaT research (Hobson et al., 2009) revealed that high emotions, whether positive or negative, are characteristic of the early career experiences of teachers. In my own experience, emotions are characteristic of the experiences of *all* teachers at whatever stage of their careers, especially when there are changes in context of whatever kind (see Chapter 1). Elsewhere (in Malderez and Bodòczky, 1999) in the short descriptions of each role, we saw this Support role as requiring the mentor to be 'a sounding-board' and to provide a 'shoulder to cry on.' I still say this and, in order for this to be possible, the quality of the relationship needs to be high. I tell my worst fears, worries and horrible mistakes to a non-judgemental friend who is a good listener, knows me well and who I trust not to spread it further, rather than to a workplace rival or boss. Similarly, I delight in my little successes and muse about what to do next to feel that good feeling again with that friend rather than risk being seen as boasting by anyone else. (This reluctance to be seen as bragging or boasting is, I realise, a result of my own background and gender, and less widespread currently, I believe, in many contexts.)

DOI: 10.4324/9781003429005-3

As the quality of the underlying mentor-mentee relationship is crucial not only for this Support role but for all your mentoring, I have chosen to begin this chapter with a focus on this relationship. I have subdivided the section according to stages in the relationship as there are specific practices and processes associated with each phase. In the Starting section, I discuss further the ideas of trust and understanding and suggest a checklist of things to do in 'First Meetings.' In 'Maintaining', I write about the adjustments that may be needed as both participants in the relationship develop and move on. The 'Ending' section includes important things to do when ending the relationship so that both parties can feel satisfied and willing and able to continue learning, and maybe in future to engage in mentoring again.

The work to understand (and 'stand under') your mentee and prove your trustworthiness, for example, will be ongoing throughout the relationship and depends, at least in part, on your ability to listen. So, I turn next to the vital listening skill needed not only in this role (to understand and stand under your mentee) but also in your Educator role (to give your mentee space to do their own careful thinking).

The chapter ends with some examples of times when, very occasionally (and in this role only, see Chapter 6), doing things *for* the mentee may be appropriate.

Your relationship

1. Starting

What follows are some ideas and suggestions for "taking the most delicate care" (Southcott et al., 2020) of the very important beginnings of your mentoring relationship. I draw on a background in group dynamics as well as my own and others' experiences of starting a new mentoring relationship.

Before, or at the same time as, starting formal mentorials, it is useful to have at least one session or chat where the sole focus is on getting to know you, for both participants. This can be incorporated into other activities in other roles (induction tours, for example, or in informal settings such as over a lunch). It is, I think, preferable to begin this 'what we have in common' task in informal settings and save the private space you will need for mentorials for your Educator role (see Chapter 6). However, when less formal opportunities have not been found, you may need to start your first more-formal session (see below) with some informal chat.

Informal chat

Even when earlier decisions regarding mentor and mentee selection and pairing are made by others, you and your mentee will still have some characteristics and experiences in common. These are a starting place for developing the kind of rapport that can lead to a productive and trusting relationship. You will both need to discover what these are, and not just assume you know what these are. At the very least, you are both teachers. Most often and ideally, you are teachers of the same subject in the same institution (or type of institution in cases where, for example, there is only one teacher of physics in a school, and you are an external mentor). In some contexts, it may have been thought important or useful for mentors and mentees to share the same gender or ethnicity or be parents, for example. Exploring what you actually have in common is a valuable topic for early informal meetings. It allows you as the mentor to begin to build a picture of where your mentee is, but also and crucially to begin trust-building.

Trust

An informal chat of the kind discussed above can help establish trust in that it requires *mutual self-disclosure* which is both one of the hallmarks of a trusting relationship and an important way of building such a relationship.

Mutual self-disclosure means that you, as mentor, will not only be finding out about your mentee, but also creating conditions where your mentee finds out about you. An initial focus on *what we have in common* not only allows for this, but also for revealing only that which is comfortable for both parties at this early stage of the relationship. Within this exploration, topics may include, for example, professional biographies, long-term professional plans and hopes, work-life balance and home contexts as well as other interests and hobbies.

As a mentor, you will need to assure your mentee of confidentiality (see 'First formal meetings'). However, it will only be over time that your trustworthiness will be proved. Your trustworthiness is crucial if you are to support your mentee's learning and development as, otherwise, your mentee will be loath to disclose and describe certain aspects of their teaching (see Chapter 6). Disclosure during an informal chat should similarly be confidential, therefore (whether or not you have already formally assured your mentee of confidentiality), it is the whole interpersonal relationship which needs to be a trusting one. If you are required to assess your mentee, you may need to specify which aspects of your relationship will/can remain confidential and which you are obliged to report to others, and how you propose to handle this duty in a way you hope will not harm your relationship or your mentee's learning (see Chapter 7).

Discovering what you have in common with your mentee not only allows for the beginning of trust-building but also of your work to understand (stand under) your mentee and begin to prove yourself as an empathetic listener and someone they could vent or talk to when they need a sounding board or use as a shoulder to cry on when/if that is necessary. As a teacher and being someone who talks-to-learn, I have always found listening in this sense a challenge! This is perhaps especially challenging when *mutual* self-disclosure is needed. I remind myself, for example, of the saying that begins "we are given one mouth but two ears", and of the need to *check my understanding* of what I have heard or of what I am beginning to understand or think I know. Periodic paraphrasing and/ or summarising is helpful for this, using sentence starters such as, "So, are you saying that…?" or "From your facial expression I'm guessing that…." (and see 'On listening' below for a brief discussion of the special type of listening required by mentors).

'Where your mentee is'

When you set out to find commonalities in your informal chat you will probably uncover clues about 'where your mentee is' on their learning teaching/learning to be a teacher journey that will be useful to reflect on and consider. While the bulk of this work will take place as a result of reflecting on mentorials (see Chapters 6 and 8), tentative 'broad-brush' hypotheses developed as an outcome of informal chats are useful starting points to refine as the work progresses. For example, you may find out that a mentee thought their ITP programme was 'too theoretical', (prompting you maybe to make a mental note regarding the importance and value, for this mentee, of step 3 in the five-step post-lesson mentorial protocol – see Chapter 6). Or it may be that information you get during a professional biographies chat leads you compare what you have heard against various ways of describing stages of teacher development over a career (see Chapter 8 and Malderez and Wedell, 2007). You may wonder whether, for example, your mentee will still be focused mainly on their own behaviours in class and in school or will have also added a focus on pupil or student behaviours, or whether they are – yet – also focusing on signs of pupil or student learning. Step 1 in the five-step process, in particular (Chapter 6), will be a time to listen carefully for evidence to test your initial hypotheses.

First formal meeting

Much, if not all, of the time allotted for your first formal mentorial meeting will be needed to establish and agree on ground rules for your work together. In particular, you will need to discuss goals and ways of working.

Goals

It is important to establish shared goals for the mentoring for three main reasons. Firstly, they can guide your work during the mentoring process. Secondly, you will need to refer back to your agreed goals to establish successes or progress at the end of the mentoring process and, depending on the duration of your mentoring, also periodically during it. Finally, being open about goals is also another opportunity for mutual self-disclosure.

After briefly explaining the need for shared goals in the mentoring partnership, an opening prompt might be, "Can you tell me a bit about why you have chosen to engage in mentoring? What are you hoping to achieve through our work together"? Mentee responses can vary. For example:

1. I just feel I need some guidance; or
2. I need to do better on my next assessment; or
3. I need someone to tell me where I'm going wrong; or
4. I want to learn how to engage students; or
5. I'm working on using groupwork/ways of dealing with errors and feel doing it with some support would be helpful; or a more general comment such as
6. I know the value of talking about teaching for my professional development and this is a great opportunity.

The examples above are ordered from the kind of responses you might expect from less- to more-experienced mentees. Responses 1 to 3 might come from beginning teachers, who lack some self-confidence and may believe that there is one right way of teaching – that you know and will tell them which will make them able to do it. Helping them realise the flaws in this argument will therefore be a focus of your work together. Responses (4) and (5) are fairly rare (in my experience) but are very helpful starting points. However, the mentee's goals are expressed, it will be important to find out about *why* your mentee has these goals. You may both subsequently discover that these are, in fact, not the most valuable learning points for your mentee's teaching at the time. Your first, or first few, post-lesson mentorials will be helpful in this regard, after which you may need to adjust agreed-upon goals. When you hear something like response (6), your main challenge may be in establishing SIRP (see Chapter 6) as a central practice.

Your goals

Mentors I know have prepared to say, for example, "as I'm new to mentoring for teacher professional development I'm keen to develop my mentoring skills in the practices I have learnt to do this. So, I'm going to need your help and I'm looking forward to learning a lot with you, not just about mentoring but about teaching too."

Or, they might say, "I'm keen to develop my mentoring skills, in particular my active listening (see below)/how to scaffold your learning, and I'm looking forward to learning a lot with you, not just about mentoring but about teaching too."

In other words, mentors need to think carefully beforehand about what they want to learn from the mentoring partnership and be as open as they feel able or believe is appropriate.

Partnership/shared goals

These are developed, worded, agreed-upon and recorded by mentee and mentor together on the understanding that they can be revisited and revised at any time.

Ways of working

This is the time to formally establish that your mentoring relationship is a *confidential* one and that nothing that is said during mentorials will be reported or otherwise passed on to others without the express consent of your mentee. In the event that you as mentor find the need to discuss with fellow mentors a particular issue you are having, you would do so anonymously if your mentee gives you permission to do so. In most instances, everything said in your chosen private mentorial space would remain within that space.

You may also want to emphasise that your role is always a *non-judgemental* one. Rather than judging, you are there to guide your mentee to making their own informed judgements and decisions.

Both of these two claims – confidentiality and being non-judgemental – will be more or less easily believed depending on your mentee's prior experiences, and perhaps on any other duties (such as those of an assessor) you are required to take on. (See Chapter 4 if you are required to also be a trainer and Chapter 7 if you have to also formally assess the person who is also your mentee.) In other words, you will need to prove yourself over time.

In talking about how you will work together, you will need to agree to a regular weekly *time and place* for the formal mentorials and explain your informal *availability* at other times of the week. Ideally, you can offer some time for brief informal exchanges. If your mentor coordinator has organised for your daily *proximity* (for example, you are both in the same staffroom or use the same staff facilities), you may need to say little more than something like, "And I'll be seeing you most days anyway so we can snatch a quick chat as/when needed. Just ask – I'll say if I can't stop then for any reason and tell you when I will be available." You may also want to share your phone number and/or email address, but it will protect you if you specify when you will and will not respond to messages and calls. We need to aim for enough *availability* in terms of informal time for the mentee to feel supported, but not so much that we risk keeping our mentee in *learned helplessness* or leave ourselves with too little time for our own teaching or other responsibilities.

In many contexts now (and because of historical mentor practices and the expectations they have given rise to), you will need to explain that observing them teaching is usually *not* something you expect to do. "I won't come and observe you teaching unless you invite me for one reason or another – certainly not at first and probably never – because what matters is what YOU notice, not what I notice." Ideally, you will be able to add, "And I'm not a trainer or an assessor" (see Chapter 7).

In some contexts, a mentor's observation of teaching is still a requirement, in which case when and why you will observe needs to be stated, understood and agreed to – if not at the first meeting, as the mentoring progresses. It *can* be helpful for two main reasons: a) preparing for a formal assessment by another (see Chapter 7), or b) when a mentee is working on learning a particular skill that is useful in the classroom and asks for another pair of eyes to help them review their progress. I wrote 'it *can* be helpful' because what makes it so is a mentor's skill and ability to remain non-judgemental in post-observed lesson discussions. This is a huge challenge – as teachers, we can't stop ourselves *having* judgements when observing another teaching. Those judgements will be based on the way-to-teach model we have developed for ourselves. Yet our mentee may be going to develop into a very different but possibly equally, or even more, effective type of teacher. Using the SIRP protocol does help, but the challenge after observed lessons comes when sharing what we noticed at Step 1. We are bound to 'notice' (and report) the unexpected/unwanted – the mistakes if you like (see On Noticing, Chapter 6) – and at some level the mentee knows this. Being factual will help and sticking to the protocol, too. However, in these contexts and because of this risk, the stronger your relationship and the longer you can delay observing the better.

If remaining time is limited but you spot evidence that your mentee is confused about how you can help them if you don't observe their teaching, you may want to simply say something like, "There are protocols we'll use for how I can guide you through a thinking process to arrive at your own decisions in pre-lesson planning and preparation as well as when reflecting on and learning from your experiences of teaching in post-lesson discussions."

Alternatively, or in addition, you could introduce, for example, the protocol for post-lesson mentorials – perhaps by simply showing/providing a printed copy. "This is the protocol we'll be using for post-lesson discussions – how I hope to support you in making your own informed judgements and decisions" (and see First mentorial, Chapter 6).

You may even have time (if an informal chat has occurred before the meeting) and goal-setting gone smoothly, for a quick 'first go' at using a protocol, but this will need at least 30 minutes and probably longer. I feel it is important to ensure that a first use of a protocol has a successful outcome (for example, the mentee *does* arrive at their own judgements and decisions and *has* worked out what to do next). So, if there is not enough time, I would postpone this for the second meeting.

I often scribble a Reminder Checklist, or skeleton plan, of topics to cover/ things to do in a First Meeting to glance at as the meeting progresses and to help ensure I remember to say and do important things. Such a checklist might look something like the list next which is mostly a summary of what I have written above. Items in parentheses may left out or postponed depending on the context. You could also, of course, develop this skeleton plan into something you find more practical to work with. Whether you use a plan or a brief checklist, I would suggest you use the pre-lesson mentorial protocol in Chapter 6, to help you in your own preparation of self particularly.

1. (Informal Chat)
2. Goal-setting
3. Ways of working

    Agree weekly time and place for mentorials
    Confidentiality, non-judgemental,
    Availability - (*see Chapter 1*)
    Mentorial language - (*see Introduction*)
    No 'observation'
       Showing/give printed copy of mentorial protocol

4. (First use of a protocol)

2. Maintaining

We spend time with, and give attention to, those people in our lives with whom we have trusting and good relationships. Friends or potential friends are often lost and relationships fizzle out when life changes mean we cannot or do not 'find the time' or it is (or feels) just impossible or not a priority to 'make the effort.' Basically, regular time spent together talking and engaging in activities that interest both participants is a big part of what maintains any interpersonal relationship. The need for 'time together' to ensure relationship maintenance is usually met on most formal mentoring scheme where regular mentorial meetings are scheduled and informal opportunities planned.

However, as in any relationship, there will be changes in each participant over time which will impact the relationship. For example, while beginning teachers in particular will benefit from many pre-lesson mentorials initially, over time you should be able to focus more on post-lesson mentorials and your mentee's learning of SIRP (see Chapter 6). More-experienced teacher-mentees – and the type that might give you goal (vi) above – will probably most benefit from most mentorials being post-lesson ones.

If your formal relationship is planned to last more than a few months, you will also need to periodically review learning and goals and agree to any adjustments to ways of working.

Your own SIRP on your mentoring practice (see Chapter 8) will be important not only for your Model role (see Chapter 4) and your own professional development, but also to allow you to make appropriate adjustments as your relationship develops and address any interpersonal tensions that may arise.

3. Ending

There are three important things to do to end the mentoring relationship in a positive way.

1.   Revisit goals and review achievements.
2.   Ensure mentees have what they need to continue their learning without a formal mentor's support.
3.   Say personal goodbyes.

Revisit goals and review achievements

In looking through the latest version of the shared goals, there will be much a mentee might want to say they have still to learn. Who can ever say they have finished learning, or that they help all their learners learn all the time? But mentors will want to keep the focus on what the mentee *has* achieved, including, for example, increased self-confidence, ability to engage in productive SIRP and so on. The mentor will also want to acknowledge the role their mentee has played in allowing them to achieve their own goals.

Ensure mentees have what they need to continue their learning without a formal mentor's support

This is a time to remind the mentee that they now have all the tools they need to continue their learning. They have learnt planning and preparation processes as well as skills to engage in SIRP which will allow them to manage their own ongoing learning. You may also want to review or note any resources they now have access to or have learnt about during the mentoring process which may continue to be useful (for example, local professional libraries, websites of professional bodies and other resources).

Say personal goodbyes

It is lovely to mark the end of the formal relationship in some way – a last lunch together as mentor and mentee, for example. In many situations, it won't be a case of reverting to 'ordinary' colleagues – in my experience, former mentees are always 'special.' But you will be spending less time together, and you need your mentee to understand your attention will be turning to another colleague.

Although you will not be as available to them from now on, let them know that you look forward to watching their successes.

On listening

Listening is one of the key skills beginning mentors (and coaches) need to develop (Malderez and Bodòczky, 1999; van Nieuwerburgh, 2020). This is because the kind of listening required is very different from what we all employ in normal conversations in both quantity and quality. In ordinary social conversations, we normally share the speaker/listener roles more or less equally. In mentoring, in your Support role – and particularly perhaps in your Educator role (Chapter 6) – you will need to be in listener mode for as much as 80% or 90% of the time. You will, however, be busy and working towards clear aims, even though you are silent. This aspect of your listening is emphasised by the term Active Listening, and we drew on the literature relating to this in our 1999 publication (Malderez and Bodòczky).

Your aims in the Support role, which include being a sounding board and a shoulder to cry on, require not only a good relationship so that your mentee is *willing* to talk to you, but also good listening skills so that your mentee *can* vent and be/feel heard for cathartic purposes. Quality listening is also required in this or other roles in order to provide space for your mentee to re-view and recall and to think more carefully and more deeply as well as to enjoy the process and feel satisfied by the outcomes.

I have recently discovered that much of the coaching literature lists 'levels' of listening (four or five) from simpler to more complex. I provide one list here, adapted by me and given in van Nieuwerburgh (2020). (My adaptations are largely just substituting the words mentor and mentee for coach and coachee!) To each level I have added my own commentary.

We suggest mentor training activities in our 1999 book (Malderez and Bodòczky) for all these levels, and I have included simple five-minute practice/awareness-raising activities in the commentaries for the first three levels below.

Level 1. Attending: mentor gives undivided attention to mentee, suggesting interest in what they have to say

Commentary

Although given as the simplest of the levels, and an everyday interpersonal skill, this is demanding enough. Try this activity with a colleague or family member:

   Agree on a topic. Face each other and take turns listening/attending to the other person speaking on that topic for one minute. (Use a stop watch for accurate timing.)

   How often did you find yourself distracted by your own internal monologue and thoughts about what you were hearing? How easy was it to fully 'attend' to the speaker and what you were hearing?

Of course, choice of topic as well as quality of the relationship itself also impact how well we can, will or indeed want to 'attend.' Even though, as a mentor, you will want to attend, you will need to attend for much longer than a minute! Practising how to let your own thoughts and 'head chatter' recede and refocus on your mentee and on understanding them and what they are saying is likely therefore to be an ongoing challenge!

Level 2. Accurate listening: mentor is able to reflect back, for example, by quoting or paraphrasing, what the mentee has said

Commentary

Accurate listening in this sense – as evidenced by whether or not the listener can accurately reflect back what the other has said – depends on more than language skills. Use of language (on both sides) has an impact as well as the level of trust in the relationship and how well participants know each other. What is important is to accurately paraphrase or summarise what the person *meant* and also to get the speaker's assessment that you have done this accurately.

> Try the one-minute listening activity (given above under Level 1) again. This time, after listening, 'reflect back' and summarise/paraphrase what you have heard in 30 seconds. Check with your partner whether or not you have 'got it right' or have listened accurately. Repeat as necessary until your partner can say, "Yes. That's exactly what I meant."
>
> How many tries did you need before your speaker agreed you had fully 'got it'? What hindered you? Was it the quality of your initial 'attending' (which can be hidden by the excuse of 'poor short-term memory'!) or the need to find accurate synonyms or umbrella terms for ideas your speaker expressed? Perhaps it was a combination?

In mentoring, there are many occasions where such reflecting back to check you have fully understood your mentee is really useful. It can help both of you. Your mentee benefits from a sense of being heard, but also from the pause in their own thinking and speaking, and even, at times, from the stimulus that the actual words you use to summarise or paraphrase can provide. It can help you, too, not only in better understanding your mentee but also in giving you a little break before you resume the hard work of active listening. "Hang on a minute, can I just check I am understanding you so far?"

Level 3. Empathic listening: mentor listens not only to the mentee's words, but also to the emotional content behind the words

This level depends to a large extent on the noticing (see Chapter 6) you do as a mentor-listener of the *way* your speaker speaks and any body-language clues they exhibit while talking, as much as on what the speaker actually says. In your Support role, you will be looking out for such things in order to gauge an appropriate response. When your mentee responds to a quick "How's it going?" with "Fine" while avoiding eye contact, sounding flat and even sighing, you may, depending on the time you have available and the stage in your relationship, want to come back with a comment. For example, "Hmmm, well, you don't sound very fine to me! Let's go for a coffee and chat about what seems to be bothering you." Or, you may say, "Ok, well, I'm here you know if you need to talk through anything." Or, you may simply want to file it away to start the next mentorial with a comment such as, "On Monday, you replied to my query about how things were going by saying 'fine.' But to me you seemed a bit flat, a bit down. Am I right? Can you identify what was causing those feelings? If it was a particular lesson you'd just had that disappointed you, shall we make that a focus of our mentorial today?" Reasons for your mentee's mood may turn out to be related to something other than classroom teaching. It may be that 'an alienator' (see Chapter 1) in your context said something unsupportive to your mentee. In that case, your role would be to reassure the mentee (and privately resolve to have a word with your colleague). If it turns out that the reason for being 'down' had something to do with your mentee's home life, for example, it is probably worth remaining in Support role and providing a shoulder to cry on, if this seems wanted or needed, before starting your formal mentorial focusing on a past or future lesson. The old saying that 'a teacher teaches themselves' not only means that teachers manage their own learning (which, in your Educator role, you will ensure your mentee is willing and able to do) but also that what a pupil learns is as much the person and attitudes and personality of the teacher. Pupils have long chosen 'enthusiasm' as a characteristic of a 'good teacher', and a teacher who is 'down' because of some life issue is unlikely to find being enthusiastic very easy. I am not suggesting a mentor in Support role needs to be a therapist, more like a good listening friend and perhaps one who can point the sufferer to a professional counsellor where needed and available.

This type of empathic listening is especially important in your Educator role at Step 1 of SIRP (Chapter 6) because spotting the emotional clues (whether of pleasure, excitement or disappointment) in your mentee's description of what happened tells you where your mentee's 'readiness to learn' is and helps you both find the focus for the mentorial.

> As a way of practising this, use the same one-minute listening activity and try to include perceptions of emotional content behind the words into your 'reflecting back' stage. For example, on a topic of 'hobbies and pastimes', you might be able to include, for example, "You seemed particularly enthusiastic when you were talking about your creative hobbies, painting and short story writing. You also mentioned walking and going to the gym, although not with the same enthusiasm."

Level 4. Pure listening: mentor can reflect back to mentee thoughts and feelings that are at the 'edge' of their awareness, that the mentee may not be fully aware of yet

Commentary

For me, this level is more an outcome of having employed high skills in the first three types of listening. In other words, I am not sure that a mentor can develop skills specifically for this other than those developed for the first three levels above, nor that it can be planned for. It just happens sometimes in contexts of real communication. This idea of 'becoming aware' of something on hearing another's careful paraphrasing or summarising of something we have said and the way we said it reminds me of a view of communication called the Johari Window of Communication, which was named after Joseph Luft and Harrington Ingham, the two psychologists who created it (see Luft and Ingham, 1955). They depict the 'window' as a square with four equal panes. The panes in the lower horizontal row are labelled, left to right, *unknown/closed* and *blind spot* and refer to aspects of ourselves that are unknown to us. The panes in the upper row are labelled *façade* (things we consciously hide from others) and *arena/open*. If we look at the window from the point of view of our listener or interlocutor, we look at the vertical columns. The panes in the column on left of the window are labelled, from top to bottom, *façade* and *closed* and are aspects of ourselves that are unknown to others. The panes in the column on the right, again labelled from top to bottom, are *arena* and *blind spot* and are aspects of ourselves that are known to others.

In real, satisfying communication, there can be movement of that which is unknown to us from our blind spots into the arena or, when we trust enough, from our façade into the arena. In some cases, even something neither of us knew can become known and move directly from the *closed* area into the *arena* or via our *blind spot* or *facade*. In other words, conversations with an interlocutor with high-level listening skills can increase our knowledge of ourselves, as people as well as teachers.

For more ways to further develop your crucial listening skills, see Chapter 8.

Doing things for your mentee

In your Educator role (see Chapter 6), you will be enacting one of the important principles of scaffolding (see Introduction): that of *not* doing 'it' for the learner (when 'it' is what is being learnt, such as making informed decisions and so on). An educator will instead provide hints and clues and other forms of guidance such as prompting the next move in the process, so that the learner does 'it' themselves. This is *hard* (I have found) for us, as we know how to do 'it' and can see, we believe, what the next step is or 'should' be. We therefore spend a lot of our formal mentoring time in mentorials biting our tongues and listening/ attending, waiting patiently and not jumping in with our ideas and suggestions.

However, there may be times in our Support role (and occasionally in other roles apart from the Educator one) when doing things for our mentee can be appropriate. This is true particularly with student- or beginning-teacher mentees. The important thing here is to ensure that what we do really is helpful for our mentee. The temptation is to do things for ourselves rather than for our mentee. As an example, planning or assessing a lesson *for* our mentee may, in a sense, help us. If nothing else, it is a lot quicker to just do it ourselves. It does not help your mentee in the long-term who is deprived of the opportunity to begin to learn the complex process of lesson planning and preparation, for example (see Chapter 6). Often it doesn't help much in the short-term either. If I use another's plan without fully understanding the thinking behind it, it is unlikely to work. The key here for when it *can* be appropriate to do things for your mentee is to take your cue from the mentee and the circumstances. See examples below.

The times when we can do something **for** our mentee in this Support role have two main characteristics:

- What we do **for** our mentee is not something they are learning (perhaps not yet specified in our goals), although you may want to suggest adapting goals as a result of the incident.
    1. Example: Mentee in pre-lesson panic. Mentor does required photocopying *for* mentee, and goals are adapted to include time management (and more pre-lesson mentorials are planned with a focus on the 'concrete preparation' phase; see Chapter 6).
- What we do **for** our mentee is in response to our assessment of their emotional state.
    2. Example: Mentee 'can't think' of an activity to do 'X' just before a lesson. Mentor makes suggestion and provides materials, and goals are adapted to include time management (and more pre-lesson mentorials are planned).

The important thing, as the examples above illustrate, is that when we **do** something **for** our mentee, it is in order to relieve our mentee's stress and because we believe it is likely to result in a more positive teaching–learning experience for the mentee and their students.

In the next chapter, I look at the second mentor role, that of Acculturator, which is needed at and from the very start of your mentoring work.

References

Claxton, G. (1997), *Hare brain, tortoise mind*. London: Forth Estate.

Hobson, A.J., Malderez, A., Tracey, L., Homer, M.S., Ashby, P.& Mitchell, N. (2009), *Becoming a teacher: teachers' experiences of initial teacher training, induction and early professional development. Final report.* DCSF Research Report DCSF-RR115. London: Department of Education and Skills.

Luft, J.& Ingham, H.(1955), *The Johari window, a graphic model of interpersonal awareness.* Proceedings of the Western training laboratory in group development. Los Angeles: UCLA.

Malderez, A. & Bodòczky, C. (1999), *Mentor courses: a resource book for trainer trainers.* Cambridge: Cambridge University Press.

Malderez, A. & Wedell, M. (2007), *Teaching teachers: processes and practices.* London: Continuum.

Southcott, J., Marangio, K., Rady, D. & Gindidis, M. (2020), "Taking the most delicate care": beginnings of a mentoring relationship between teachers and coaches in an Australian school. *The Qualitative Report*, Vol. 25, No. 7, pp.19905-1918.

van Nieuwerburgh, C. (2020), *An introduction to coaching skills: a practical guide.* London: Sage.

3 Mentor Role 2: Acculturator

Helping your mentee adjust to the school and the profession

This short chapter considers ways you may be able to help your mentee join or adjust to various professional communities. Such communities range from local groups in the school or institution to national and international professional associations. Joining fully or remaining on the periphery of the local groups inevitably comes with the job. Your Acculturator role aims to support your mentees in becoming full contributing members of such groups, rather than to mould your mentee to fit the group, such that they become co-creators of the developing culture. In other words, mentees are not blank sheets, they come with valuable knowledge, thoughts and experiences to offer the group. In addition, membership in professional associations is one hallmark of what it means to be a professional (and see Chapter 4), and a mentor will often also want to enable membership in such associations.

This chapter addresses preparatory thinking tasks for this Acculturator role and describes some ways others have acted as a result.

1. What professional associations are available and useful for me as well as my mentee?

A way to begin is to list the professional communities you yourself belong to and have benefitted from. These are the ones you will be able to help your mentee join if and when appropriate. You could map these on a cline from local to global or place them in concentric circles with the 'local' groups in the centre.

For example, at one point fairly early in my career, my own cline might have looked something like this:

Local _____ National _____ Global
Teachers in my staffroom
Teachers (Ts) in my department and institution
                    Technical college teachers.   International
                                                         Association of
                                                         TEFL

DOI: 10.4324/9781003429005-4

2. How would you characterise the communities and associations you yourself belong to or are familiar with?

Apart from local communities, there are many different kinds of professional associations in teaching. Such associations in teaching usually have a membership with specific shared characteristics:

- They may focus on the age of the pupil. Examples of these would be associations of teachers of young or primary age pupils or associations of teachers of adults.
- There are associations for most taught subjects, such as for science or language teachers.
- There are associations for teachers in particular institutional settings; for example, for teachers in primary, secondary and tertiary education.
- There are associations of teachers in particular geographical contexts, whether local or global.
- There are associations for researchers of teaching, practitioners and practitioner-researchers.

The main characteristic or characteristics of the expected membership are usually expressed in the name of the association. However, many will incorporate several of the above aspects. In particular, the balance between 'research' and 'practice', however defined, will vary.

You may also belong to one or more online communities you trust and have found helpful which you could also introduce to your mentee.

Later in my career, my own cline expanded. I became a member of various associations that are more research-focused. Although these benefitted me at the time, I considered they were not the most useful organizations for a beginning teacher mentee to join.

3. What communities or professional associations might my mentee be familiar with?

Thinking about what you already know about your mentee, consider which of the communities on your own cline your mentee might already have joined. Even if you have yet to meet your mentee, the design and purpose of the mentoring scheme you will be working in is a starting point. For example, if you are a mentor for a student teacher or a beginning teacher, your mentee may not be a member of (m)any associations or professional communities.

When mentees are student teachers or **beginning teachers**, they are unlikely to have yet joined any professional community. In this context, and although your focus will inevitably be on the 'local' and therefore 'must join' communities (see Induction as Acculturation below), there will probably be opportunities for you to at least make your mentee aware of useful groups towards the 'global' end of the cline. For example, you may be able to mention a journal of an association as the source of an idea you contribute in Steps 3 or 6 of the SIRP protocol (see Chapter 6). If you have a meeting or conference coming up for one of the more practice-oriented communities you belong to, try to take your mentee with you as a participant or even a co-presenter. This is an invaluable strategy which helps you fulfil both your Acculturator and Model roles (see Chapter 4). One of my student teachers/mentees co-presented with me at a national subject-focused conference with a mentoring strand. Having also chosen other presentations to attend, she dashed around from room to room all day and later reported excitedly on the many ideas she had gleaned. She also exclaimed enthusiastically, "I want to be in your gang!"

Mentees who are **more-experienced teachers** fall into two groups: those who are new to the institution and those who are not.

Experienced teachers who are long-standing colleagues will probably not need much support from you in this role. However, you might usefully look out for opportunities to introduce them to any associations you are a member of at the global end of the cline which you know they have not joined.

Experienced teachers who are new to the institution will probably need as much induction to the institution and support in joining local communities as beginning teachers. This may feel a bit patronising – they are experienced teachers after all. However, ways of working, cultures and quirks can vary hugely from one institution to another even at the level of language and terms used for what may be familiar practices. When I was an experienced teacher in a new job, my induction consisted largely of being quickly shown around the premises. Emails arrived periodically with notices about upcoming 'board' meetings. I ignored them as I believed I was a lowly member of staff, not a board member. After some months, a colleague told me, "You know it's frowned on not to attend board meetings." "But I'm not a board member!" I exclaimed. "Yes, you are," was the reply. At my puzzled look, an explanation was offered: "It's our 'staff meeting,' if you like."

Induction as acculturation

Whatever the form of any formal induction your mentee has had and whether or not you were involved, it is helpful to view this phase of joining local communities as a process. I expect we have all experienced those induction days where we emerge in the fog of information-overload. At a minimum, a mentor can helpfully field resultant queries or provide reminders. A mentor's role can also include one or more of the following over a number of weeks:

- showing the mentee around the premises, with a particular focus on places a mentee will need or want to visit often.
- explaining any conventions associated with using spaces. For example, you may need to say something like, "You can grab a coffee any time, and there's an honesty box here. Most people bring their own mugs, and some get quite upset if anyone else uses their mug. There are a few white ones at the end there for anyone to use."
- going *with* your mentee to at least the first few regular community events; for example, staff meetings, interest groups, training days and so on.
- encouraging or inviting your mentee to speak up and offer their perspectives and suggestions in community gatherings and model appreciation of their contributions.
- introducing the mentee to all members of local communities and providing information about the person just introduced, such as:
    - how she/he fits into a system ("She's the deputy head of X, responsible for Y");
    - where their staffroom/desk is ("His office is next to reception"); and
    - whether and in what circumstances your mentee might need to find them ("You're unlikely to come across her very often, but if you're concerned about the attendance of a student, for example, she'd be the first person to turn to").

In summary, as a mentor preparing for this Acculturator role, there are three main things you will need to consider:

- the communities your mentees are joining, and must become full members of, by virtue of their job;
- those communities and associations they could potentially join which might be helpful to their professional development; and
- what you personally can do in this role/to fulfil this role.

The roles of a mentor's practice (Chapters 2 to 6) are interconnected. I expect you have already realised that opportunities for 'informal chats' (see chapter 2) abound while also fulfilling your Acculturator role. Similarly, you will notice further connections and overlaps with this role and the next, the Model role.

4 Mentor Role 3: Model

Modelling professionalism

A mentor's main duty in this third role relates to modelling what it means to be a professional teacher. I do not mean you need to be perfect. No professional ever is. We are human, and uncertainties and 'failures' (learning opportunities?!) are part of the life of any professional. I do mean that you will need to reveal and make visible how you deal with these and other aspects of professionalism for your mentee to notice. A mentee will then have a model not only of *how* you do things (reflect, work on your own learning and so on – see below) but also that you do regularly engage in these aspects of professionalism. We cannot claim that there is one 'right' way of in-class teaching. Everything is context-dependent (see Chapter 1). Therefore, a mentor will rarely need or want to model (any aspect of) 'how to teach.' As one mentor I worked with once said, "My mentee shouldn't become a second me, but a more enriched herself."

In this chapter, the various aspects of what it means to be a professional are outlined, and the challenges of this model role are discussed for each aspect. As always, you will find lists of practical strategies others have used to try to overcome these challenges. Lastly, I list some situations when modelling some teaching Know How might be appropriate and other situations when caution is needed.

What any professional (for example, doctor, lawyer, teacher) does and is

Apart from broadly similar preparation procedures for their job (extensive university-level education and internship phases), the hallmarks of all professionals are that they:

- manage their own ongoing learning and make their own informed decisions and judgements;
- keep up to date;
- belong to one or more professional bodies;
- maintain context-appropriate standards of behaviour, dress and speech; and
- are paid and are therefore accountable.

DOI: 10.4324/9781003429005-5

I now look at each of these in turn and list possible strategies to overcome the modelling challenges for each.

Manage their own ongoing learning and make their own informed decisions and judgements

This is a core aspect of professionalism and one which is almost entirely invisible to others. It is also one that some contexts can make difficult to achieve. Such contexts are those which micromanage teachers, treating them as technicists rather than professionals, often justifying this as attempts to 'raise standards', requiring certain 'best practices' in all situations, for example. However, even if you find yourself in this situation, it will be crucial for you to model this aspect of professionalism, especially as this is a core practice that the mentor is helping the mentee learn (see Chapter 6). In my experience, even contexts which are overly prescriptive and controlling claim to aspire to a professional workforce and explicitly mention reflective practice in their documents.

The main challenge for any mentor in modelling this aspect of professionalism – achieved mainly through private reflective practice – is how to make what is usually invisible visible.

Some strategies mentors have used to make their modelling of this aspect of professionalism visible include the following ideas.

- Sharing summaries of their own reflective practice on their own teaching at appropriate moments. "I had this problem with one class and on reflection, after considering lots of possibilities, I decided it could be to do with X. So, I searched and found this article on X with useful practical ideas for what to do. I decided to plan them into the next lesson and it seemed to work – well, it was a lot better! I'm still working on it."
- Inviting the mentee into one of their own classes to be another pair of eyes because they were working on X or Y. After the lesson, the mentor talked aloud as a mentee would and worked through the five-step process. In a role-reversal, this person invited the mentee to contribute what they noticed at Step 1. After they had generated their own ideas, the mentor also invited their mentee to contribute any ideas they might have at later steps of the protocol described in Chapter 6. This allowed the mentor to model their own skills in the SIRP they were helping the mentee learn, as well as demonstrate that it is a part of any professional's practice.
- Seeking permission to record a mentorial in order to help them review their mentoring practice and manage their own ongoing learning of mentoring. (See also Chapter 8 for several ways recordings of mentorials can both support different aspects of your own development as a mentor and provide modelling opportunities.)

Keep up to date

This core aspect of what it means to be a professional is also often invisible to your mentee.

A perceptive mentee might notice, for example, your references to certain journals, websites or books where you have found useful ideas. However, why and when you sought out these ideas and how they affected your own learning and practice will probably be invisible to the mentee. The challenge again is to make this visible.

A frequent strategy used is to explain the context in which you came to find the sources relevant and useful to you (and see above).

Your attendance at 'training days' or conferences and talking about the useful 'nuggets' you have gained also help your modelling of this aspect.

Belong to one or more professional bodies or associations

Again, this may not be an aspect of your professionalism that is easily visible to a mentee.

Journals you consult or refer to, and which are associated with particular associations you belong to, can provide an opportunity to explain the association and why you chose to become a member.

Taking your mentee to a conference with you (see Chapter 3) is another strategy.

Maintain context-appropriate standards of behaviour, speech and dress

It is this aspect of professionalism that is frequently meant when people complain about others, saying things like "she/he isn't very professional," because this aspect is easily visible to others. Something 'she/he' has done, said or worn has differed from contextual norms. Not only is it easily visible, but the 'different' is one of the easiest things *to* notice. (See Chapter 6.) So, it is unsurprising that it is the one most commented on (criticised) by others. Despite being the easiest to spot though, it is usually not (or rarely – see my stories below) the most important part of what it means to be a professional.

Speech and behaviour

In part, speech or behaviours that are or are not acceptable can be an issue of cultures or acculturation. See my 'board meetings' anecdote regarding language in the previous chapter.

What follows are some anecdotes from my personal experience. I start with two stories which I personally found both unprofessional and shocking.

In some countries, I've found that hitting pupils is still widely practised and seemed to be acceptable for most. In one such context, as mentor, I suggested – exceptionally (see Chapter 6 Yes buts and What ifs) – that the starting point for a systematic reflection process should be the hitting incident – the pupil's behaviour which had led to the teacher-mentee hitting the pupil as response. By the end of this process, the mentee had not only found some possible alternative ways of thinking about and responding to such pupil behaviour, but the mentee also was musing on the possible connections between adults using their superior physical power and violence in classrooms to dominate and control pupils and the recent civil war, where the dominant, more powerful group had used violence to control and subdue the less powerful group in their country.

In too many places around the world, the negative labelling of pupils to their face or in staffrooms is rife. It happened to my own child in one country we lived in. He told me he was upset because his teacher had called him a name (meaning something like an idiot) in class. My strategy here was to meet and empathise with my son's teacher having to try to teach a language class of so many levels, with pupils like my son who were beginners and others who had already had two or three years of learning the language. I invited her to join our teachers' group where upcoming sessions were on 'mixed-level teaching' and 'expressing high expectations' (which included avoiding negative labels, though I didn't tell her that then). She joined us. My son was never publicly insulted in class again as far as I know!

In both these instances, I was somewhat discomfited by possible imperialist overtones in my behaviour. Who was I to question cultural norms? However, I reasoned that I had to remain true to my own values and that I had, anyway, been invited into these contexts to bring a different perspective.

Incidentally, you probably noticed my judgemental use of the words 'too many' at the start of the second story above. I, of course, easily noticed those aspects of behaviour that differed from my own views on appropriate professional standards and have revealed my judgements through my choices of examples as well as language!

My last example is related more to context and cultural norms that, once I was aware of them, I could accommodate. This story concerns norms on being punctual (or not). When I worked in the south of England, I would, when I could, get to my classroom before the students in order to set up the room – for example, moving desks and chairs to enable group-work or putting up posters and other visual aids. Starting lessons on time, punctually, was part of expected professional behaviour, and I didn't want to use up time at the start of the lesson moving furniture about and so on. When I then worked in China and tried to do the same thing, I got to the classroom early but found all the students already there. I then arrived even earlier and saw the consternation of students who arrived after me (all of us before the official start of the lesson). I learnt I had to tell the class monitor how to set up the room, and then arrive on time, or even one or two minutes late, in order to allow students to save face and politely be there waiting for their teacher.

Your context may have a written code of conduct, which you may need to communicate to your mentee. Whether such a document exists or not, in this mentor role you need to exemplify context-appropriate standards of conduct – at least those that don't conflict with your values.

Dress

In my first job in a secondary school on the east coast of England, I remember being told that wearing trousers for female teachers was unacceptable. This caused me problems in drama lessons. As a short person, I was used to hopping on a chair to see over the heads of my pupils and doing so in skirts risked indecency, so I stayed on the floor and missed, I am sure, some antics my lanky pupils engaged in at the back of the room. It also caused me problems in language lessons when I would spend a considerable amount of time on my knees in order to be at eye level, rather than tower over groups of students as they worked: tights were shredded and knees studded with splinters. Later, on a Mediterranean island, my colleagues looked to me as if they were attending a New Year's Eve party. There was so much glitter and so many sequins, high heels and short skirts – none of which I considered professional or practical work attire for a teacher. In that context it was acceptable, even expected. I conformed as much as I felt I could, aiming for 'smart', but without the high heels, short skirts, glitter or sequins. My father wore a suit and tie and university gown to teach at the grammar school when I was young, and the practical 'smart casual' dress code that is now common in many places for teachers would have been totally unacceptable then.

Your mentee will probably have noticed the dress code in your context for themselves. But again, apart from ensuring you are yourself more or less conforming to it (or explaining where or why you have challenged it), you might need to point to the relevant part of the written code of conduct, if it exists, or mention it.

Are paid, and are therefore accountable

You, or more likely your mentee, may have an official or formal 'observation and assessment' event during the course of your mentoring. At such events the assessor may be, for example, a line manager, tutor from an ITP programme, or member of some national inspectorate.

This can allow you to make the point that because professional teachers are paid, though often not enough, usually by the state, they are therefore accountable. It is normal that a paymaster will want to check that they are getting what they pay for or work out what more they need to do to ensure that they *will* get what they think they are paying for. If it is you being observed, it provides an opportunity for you to model your calm acceptance of the situation. This is true even when what paymasters think they want to see is not what you, as a professional teacher who knows your context and class best, believes they *should* be wanting! Part of what makes you able to display calm acceptance is the knowledge that whatever observers notice in your class says more about them as people, and perhaps your system, than it does about your teaching and your in-class actions to support pupil learning (and see Chapters 6 and 7).

When you might find it appropriate to model (an aspect of) teaching

The main reason you may feel you need to model an aspect of teaching is when your mentee has identified a gap in their Know How for their in-class behaviour.

In this case, you will be taking on a 'trainer' role, too (see Introduction).

There are a few situations when modelling an aspect of teaching – some of your own Know How – may be appropriate. Where you can, though, it may be preferable to arrange for your mentee to observe one or more colleagues who are known for being particularly skilled in this aspect of teaching. This allows you to remain a mentor and model of being a professional teacher (rather than a model of *teaching*). It has the added advantage, where more than one colleague is observed, of providing different experiences, even when there is one accepted 'right way' of doing something. It may also be possible and enough to talk your mentee through steps or demonstrate in mentorials (after Step 5) how to give instructions or use an interactive white board, for example, and subsequent post-lesson mentorials can track a mentee's progress in developing skills in this aspect of teaching.

So let's now look at some specific situations where you may want to consider modelling an aspect of your own teaching Know How.

With Beginning Teachers

A beginning teacher identifies an aspect of teaching Know How (in SIRP Step 5, see Chapter 6) as being something they need to learn.

- Know How, or skill development learning, begins with observation of skilled practitioners.
- Identification of steps follows the observation phase. For example, for 'giving instructions in English as Foreign Language Teaching': first, get pupils' attention; next give the instruction in short simple language; repeat, paraphrase if signs of confusion noted; demonstrate – you with able pupil or ask one pair/group to demonstrate; check understanding by asking pupils what

they have to do now; give the signal to begin; check all pupils are in fact doing what you asked; go to pairs or groups having difficulties or who are not doing as you asked; and, if necessary or many pupils are not doing what they were asked to do, pause the activity and begin the instruction-giving process again.

- After this phase of identification of steps, a mentee will need repeated attempts at 'getting it right.' Mentorials using a post-lesson protocol (see Chapter 6) can track progress and allow the mentee to identify for themselves where they 'went wrong' (usually missing a step, for example, failing to get attention or failing to prepare a short, simple instruction) and note the impact whether positive or negative. Pre-lesson mentorials can allow the mentee to prepare for their next attempt. (See Chapter 6.)

Incidentally, if your mentee is working on a piece of know-how development and invites you to do so, this can be a more legitimate occasion for a mentor-as-trainer to observe a mentee's lesson and useful in contexts where a mentor's observations of their mentee's teaching are a requirement although you will need to be very careful about remaining non-judgemental in subsequent discussions (see Chapters 6 and 7 for more details).

With more-experienced teachers

The process is the same for more-experienced teachers as for beginning teachers. The difference in my experience is in the type and amount of Know How development needed (usually less than with beginning teachers).

The process starts again with a more-experienced teacher identifying an aspect of teaching Know How in Step 5 as being something they need to learn. This will often, in my experience, be related to either using a particular piece of technology or a specific activity type which is advocated or expected in the context, rather than to more fundamental general teaching skills for which an experienced teacher will have already developed their own strategies. Observation of colleagues can again provide the first step in this discrete Know How development, or you may have to invite your mentee into your class. You will then need to provide opportunities for the subsequent steps in Know How development to occur.

When you might choose to invite your mentee to observe your class

There are a few situations where you may choose to be the model for the start of a mentee-identified piece of Know How development. These can include one or more of the following situations when:

- you intend to also use your mentee's observation of your class as a way to make your own informed reflective practice visible (see above);

- you feel your mentee's observation of your class could also enhance your credibility; and/or
- you want to make yourself vulnerable – as the class will inevitably be less than perfect – in order to enhance your relationship with your mentee.

There are some contexts in which observation of the mentor's classes is an obligatory starting point for the school-based strand of teacher preparation programmes. In such situations, it is helpful to make the pupils the focus of the post-observation discussions and support your mentee in understanding the pupils' responses and reactions. You can also arrange for your mentee to shadow those same students through their school day in other classes. This is especially useful when the mentee will be taking over the teaching of those pupils. Although they will have to forge their own relationship with the class and develop their own style of teaching, keeping some of the routines you will have established or ways of enacting schoolwide policies on pupil 'behaviour management', for example, can ease the transition for the pupils.

When you might actively avoid inviting your mentee into your class

If you have the choice, there is one specific situation when *not* inviting your mentee into your own class might be the best option. This is when your student-teacher or beginning-teacher mentee seems to still believe that there is a right way of teaching and that you know it and do it, and if you just tell them or show them, they will be able to do it, too. This is a fairly common situation early in the mentoring relationship with such mentees.

Attempting to copy models is inevitable in the early stages of learning to teach. We all start with a vision of what teaching looks like (see, for example, Lortie's 1975 'apprenticeship of observation'), and observing current teaching from the outside rather than relying on memories from their own school days (whether consciously or not; see 'Modes of mind', Chapter 8) is helpful, too. However, too much observation of just *your* teaching can send the message that you expect them to copy all you do, that you are aiming to turn them into clones. Such mentees *do* come to realise that there are so many options and that they have to build their own way of working for themselves, using their own personality, knowledge and skills. This occurs mainly after/as a result of two things. The first is careful work on your relationship such that you are seen as a professional colleague still working on your own development, rather than as 'teacher who knows it all.' This may be particularly important in contexts where, explicitly or not, criteria for mentor selection include having a reputation of being good at teaching. The second is patiently working on building your mentee's confidence in making their own decisions and judgements over time (see Chapter 6). At this point, inviting your mentee into your class becomes an option for you again.

In the next chapter, I look briefly at the Sponsor role, before turning, in Chapter 6, to the central Educator role.

Reference

Lortie, D. (1975), *Schoolteacher: a sociological study*. London: University of Chicago Press.

5 Mentor Role 4: Sponsor

Using your knowledge and contacts to help your mentee

In this chapter, I turn to the Sponsor role. In general, being a sponsor means using any power you have in the service of your mentee rather than for your own gain. Power, as in the ability to make things happen, can be accrued if we have one or more of three things: money, knowledge and good relationships with powerful others (also known as social capital or guanxi, depending on context). Being a sponsor in mentoring relates to using two of those three things – your knowledge and contacts – to help your mentee. This chapter provides specific examples of how this role could be, and has been, enacted.

I'll start with an example from my own experience. I would now say that Rod Bolitho, the Head of Department (HoD) in one of my first jobs, took a mentoring approach to his leadership of staff development. He was not called a mentor and, as a line manager of a whole department, could not have been one in the sense used in this book (see Introduction). However, on reflection, for many of us he also enacted the Support, Acculturator and Model roles as well as the Sponsor role.

It could be said he sponsored us all in providing ample opportunities for staff development. He enabled the creation of teacher development groups of peers, encouraged conference participation, urged colleagues to visit each other's lessons and so on. We did not work with textbooks as there were none considered suitable for our context, so we made our own worksheets and lesson plans, supported by the collaborative ethos of our staffroom.

Apart from using his power to enable rich staff development opportunities, there are two further personal examples I can remember which have had a lasting impact on me.

Firstly, on two separate occasions, Rod lent me books on education: a Carl Rogers book (Freedom to Learn, 1983) and a Guy Claxton book (Live and Learn, 1984). They were a departure from my usual teaching-related reading matter. Various collections of practical teaching activities to incorporate into my lessons, which we termed 'recipe books', were my usual bedtime reading matter. My own copies of both the Rogers and the Claxton book, which I subsequently bought, are still on my shelves. Since that first introduction, I have had a career-long relationship-at-a-distance with both authors and have read a lot of what they have

DOI: 10.4324/9781003429005-6

both written. I know their work will challenge my thinking and contain practical theories and ideas I can and do use in my own reflections (see Chapter 8).

Secondly, a publisher looking for writers for a coursebook suitable for a context like ours approached Rod hoping he would agree to write it. Instead, he introduced the publisher to his staff. The volunteers, a 'gang of four' women, which included a relatively inexperienced me, then set out on a journey which led to our first books (Fast Forward, 1986). That journey, in turn, brought us into contact with others. Because of that book, we went to our first international conference, for example. We also got to know a very well-known professor in our field, the late Professor Christopher Candlin. We spent a long weekend with Chris, paid for by the publisher. We discussed our drafts which we had derived from our worksheets and lesson plans, and all four of us felt we had learnt so much from our time with him. This experience was part of the reason I eventually decided to spend my first royalties on a master of education degree and was, I think, the first time I really saw the practicality of 'theory.' And it all started with Rod's sponsorship as HoD.

You may have acquired some ideas of what you might be able to do to fulfil your Sponsor role from the story above. I'll summarise below some of what others have done to use their power, in terms of knowledge and contacts – not for their own gain but for their mentee's.

Using your contacts

The fact that you, as a senior member of staff, have a good relationship with managerial staff, for example, may mean that interceding with one of them on your mentee's behalf will be beneficial for the mentee at that time. You may choose to speak to your HoD to obtain a desk in your staffroom for your mentee, for example, so that you can better fulfil your Support role (if your mentor scheme coordinator has not already done so). Or you may lobby the bursar to obtain funds for your mentee to attend a conference to fulfil part of your Acculturator role. However, how much protection or shielding and help (in the sense of doing it for them) your mentee will benefit from in the long term depends on where your mentee is in their learning teaching journey. We all need to develop our own contacts after all. The challenge for a mentor is therefore to use their contacts in ways that do not promote a learned helplessness in the mentee but are genuinely supportive.

As in my story above, you will probably also have one or two important author-contacts whose work has influenced your practice and with whom you have a relationship-at-a distance. So, as well as judiciously sharing the knowledge you have gained and use from reading their work (see below), you will also want to 'introduce' your mentee to them as important contacts of your own too.

Using your knowledge

When carrying out other mentor roles

Mentors share various types of knowledge in roles other than the Educator role (see Chapters 2 to 4).

For example, in your Acculturator role, you will be sharing what you know about people, places and procedures in your context.

When carrying out your Educator role

The important thing with being generous and sharing the Know About knowledge you have is to work out what part of the knowledge you will share, and to time it right. In other words, we need to share what we know when the mentee can hear it and make the best use of it. (See 'scaffolding' in the Introduction.) The next chapter suggests protocols for formal mentorials in which you are guided with regards to when, why and how you can contribute what you know so that it becomes an appropriate stepping stone for your mentee. This ensures that what you contribute will be perceived as relevant by your mentee.

It is not easy to restrain ourselves, partly because what we contribute will inevitably be much less than we know. We may feel we need to demonstrate our expansive knowledge in order to gain credibility, for example, but if so, we need to ask ourselves whether this would truly be using our power *in the service* of our mentee. Restraint also requires patience and trust in our mentee and their learning process. It is so hard to remember how it felt when we didn't know and the time and struggles it took us to learn! The next chapter is devoted to this Educator role and is a rather long one.

It is not only the length of its chapter which makes the Educator role different from the other roles. Most of you reading this will only need some information for roles 1 to 4 and some ideas for how you could fulfil them. You will, as professional teachers, already have most of the main knowledge and skills you need to fulfil these roles. Having said that, most of us can benefit from further active listening and interpersonal skills development, too (see Chapters 2 and 8). But the Educator role in mentoring usually requires the development of completely new and complex skills, which take time to acquire, and the embodiment of a genuinely non-judgemental approach, which can take even longer. This is partly because few of us have had the benefit of the experience of being mentored in the sense meant in this book. As it is experiential knowledge that can make something feel right to do or say, *not* 'doing as we were done unto' is horribly challenging in the moment, however convinced intellectually we are, for example, of the arguments for being non-judgemental. Here is an example of the power of experiential learning from my personal life. As a working parent

I had decided I would never tell my children to 'go away and play', as my very busy teacher mother had once done, much to my chagrin at the time. Yet I heard those very words pass my lips while trying to concentrate on lesson-planning. I was shocked! I recalled that I had, as a dismissed child, then resorted to the company of my favourite characters in a book series I was fond of at the time. That habit of reading was a gift. I realised I now understood her situation better and I forgave my mother. I also forgave myself but resolved to find out why it had happened when I had consciously resolved never to say those words. Claxton once again gave me a way forward (see Chapter 8, 'Modes of mind').

So, whether or not you are reading this book as part of a formal mentor preparation programme, I would urge you to find at least one other colleague-mentor to work with. Agree to read the next chapter before meeting. At your meeting, practise together using the protocols described in the chapter – carefully, faithfully and step by step – taking turns undertaking the mentor role. Meet and practise as many times as you need, until you both feel comfortable with your mentor role, referring perhaps to 'yes, but' sections of the chapter when needed. Your mentor role during the mentorials described in Chapter 6 does require you to be able to relax and trust the process, handing over the hard thinking work to your mentee in the belief, for example, that they can and will by the end of the process make their own informed judgements, decisions and plans. This is something that you are unlikely to be able to do very easily without personal *experiences* that prove that you can, indeed, trust the process.

References

Black, V., McNorton, M., Malderez, A. & Parker, S. (1986), *Fast forward: classbook*. Oxford: Oxford University Press.

Claxton, G. (1984), *Live and learn: an introduction to the psychology of growth and change*. London: Longman.

Rogers, C. (1983), *Freedom to learn for the 80s*, 2nd edition. New York: Merrill.

6 Mentor Role 5: Educator

Helping the mentee learn and learn to learn teaching

The Educator role encompasses anything done specifically to support a teacher learning the practice of teaching and does not (only) mean telling the mentee things (see 'Introduction: On the notion of "help"').

This chapter describes some of the main activities mentors use when in this Educator role. It starts by describing ways of managing formal mentor-mentee meetings, or mentorials, which are arguably at the heart of the mentor role. The chapter also includes a way of providing evidence of productive activity to others (managers, inspectors) without compromising the mentor-mentee relationship and ends with a list of other possible activities a mentee might choose to undertake, which may require the mentor's support as proposer or organiser.

Further short sections may follow the description of each activity as appropriate. These:

- provide an expanded rationale for the form of the activity with further detail and research support; and/or
- detail and discuss some of the typical reservations mentors have put forward when contemplating using an activity as described; and/or
- provide further explanations or descriptions, especially in relation to different contexts and aspects of 'variation.'

Each type of mentorial is described in its established and ideal form. In other words, the contexts of the descriptions are trusting mentor-mentee relationships (see Chapter 2) where both parties are familiar with the formats or protocols and have already experienced the value of working this way. In the Variations of context sections which follow, I have provided descriptions of what some mentors have done in order to establish these routines.

The first half of this chapter describes arguably the most important activity, one which is not only crucial to fulfilling your Educator role, but also at the heart of being a mentor (and of *not* being a judgementor). It is also the activity which mentors-to-be find the most challenging to learn and enact, in part because they are unlikely to have experienced it as mentees. However, if you do no more than conduct post-lesson mentorials in the way described here, you will

DOI: 10.4324/9781003429005-7

be supporting learning in so many ways. Many, even most, of the other mentor activities described in this book are about creating the conditions for these mentorials to achieve their full powerful potential.

1. Post-lesson mentorial

Aims

- To support the development of the mentee's noticing skills.
- To help the mentee see the relevance of 'theory' learnt elsewhere to their own practice and experience in schools.
- To scaffold (see Introduction) the mentee in making their own informed decisions and judgements.
- To ensure that the mentee leaves the mentorial with their own practical ideas and plans for future teaching and for developing their teaching and noticing skills.

And partly as a result of achieving these main aims, also:

- To scaffold the mentees' development of an integrated knowledge base (IKB, see Introduction) through the learning of SIRP (see Introduction).
- To support the development of teacher learnacy (Claxton, 2004).

Materials

None are essential. **Optional**: Mentorial record sheet (see section 3. Mentorial Record Sheet Completion).

Timing

Regularly, after the mentee's experiences of teaching. Ideally, the mentor will *not* have observed the lesson discussed, in part in order to make a mentor's prompts genuine and authentic.

Time needed

+/- 1 hour

Procedure

The table below describes the procedure when both mentor and mentee are used to conducting the mentorial in this way. The first two boxes in each column describe the general behaviour of each participant during the whole SIRP process, whereas the subsequent boxes describe the activities of each participant in each step of the process. The table is followed by a list of possible initial mentor prompts for each step. These are essential when the mentee is *learning* to think in this way and are also frequently needed in some form, however familiar participants are with the process, in order to keep the mentee 'on track' or achieve a satisfying conclusion within the time available.

Mentee	Mentor
The mentee leads the discussion following the five steps. During the process, the mentee may choose to invite ideas (as indicated below) from the mentor. This process helps mentees first recall and make sense of what was noticed and then use insights from their experience and what they and others (including authors in 'the literature') *know about* in order to arrive at their own judgements and decisions about what to do next for their own and their pupils' learning.	The mentor listens well, asks for clarification if she/he needs to and only offers ideas (not judgements) if/when invited by the mentee.
Step 1: What happened? Selects a lesson and part/an aspect of that lesson to work on. Describes (re-views, 'sees again'), in as much detail as she/he can, a moment from a lesson (one which causes the mentee some kind of emotional response – likely to be a perceived successful, problematic or puzzling one). Tries to help the mentor 'see' the full picture.	Listens actively (see Chapter 2, 'On listening') and tries to make a 'mental video.' When the mentee pauses or has finished describing the chosen moment, asks any questions she/he needs to in order to get that full picture. In so doing, helps develop the mentee's skill of noticing (Mason, 2002). See also 'Rationale' in this section.
Step 2: How can I understand this? Lists as many possible explanations as she/he can for what happened (for the 'success', the 'problem' or the 'puzzle'). Does not censure any thoughts at this stage and tries to make as long a list as she/he can. May choose to invite the mentor to add any other explanations she/he can think of.	Listens actively (and perhaps, after making clear what she/he proposes to do and why to gain the mentee's agreement, makes notes of ideas on the list). If invited, adds any ideas of possible interpretations/ explanations she/he can think of.

(Continued)

(Continued)

Mentee	Mentor
Step 3: What else do you know?	
a) Now tries to remember what others have said or written about the issue(s). When the mentoring is linked to a specific training or teacher education programme, explicitly tries to remember anything she/he has learnt that might be connected. b) Adds what more she/he knows about the context: the pupils, class and school that may be relevant. May choose to invite the mentor to remind him/her, or add any other relevant 'theories', books or articles or conversations that the mentor can think of.	Listens actively and patiently. If invited, adds any ideas she/he has.
Step 4: Most likely explanation?	
Thinks (aloud) about everything from steps 2 and 3 and decides what she/he thinks is the most likely explanation or interpretation of the puzzle, success or problem. Displays 'robust reasoning'/gives more than one reason for choice. May choose to check with the mentor that the reasoning seems logical.	Listens to follow the mentee's argument. If invited, asks questions about any difficulties she/he had in following the argument.
Step 5: So, what now?	
Assumes the (agreed, informed) explanation is correct, and now thinks about what that means. Considers the following: a) How exactly she/he will take account of it in the next lesson with those pupils. b) Whether it has any implications for the mentee's own learning, and if so, how she/he will manage that learning. c) Whether it has any implications for his/her noticing, and if so, how can she/he can set himself/herself to do and record that noticing. Again, after having tried (or while trying) to make these decisions, the mentee may choose to use the mentor as a resource: for practical ideas or to check the logic of the reasoning and planning.	Listens and, if necessary, prompts the mentee to consider a, b or c, if they haven't already done so. If invited, adds any ideas she/he has. (The mentor will always try to avoid giving advice or other forms of judgements, including praise, but may choose to draw the mentee's attention to the fact that she/he has successfully worked out for himself/herself some 'next steps to try', for example).

Possible initial mentor prompts

Step 1: "Ok so talk me through what happened – help me see the detail. Remember, describe things and try not to jump to interpretations or judgements just yet."

Step 2: "Now what possible explanations can you think of for that. . . . ok and? . . . . "

Step 3: "What do you know about those topics? What have you learnt (in your course) about those topics that might help you decide which of your possible explanations is the most likely? What else do you know about your pupils or your school or other aspects of your context which might help you decide?"

Step 4: "So, given all that, which do you think is the most likely explanation and why?"

Step 5: "Ok, so let's assume you are right about your explanation(s). What now? [Remember, think about your teaching, your learning and your noticing. a) How might this make a difference to what you do in the next lesson with that class? b) Is there anything you now realise you want to learn more about or learn how to do? How will you go about that? c) Given your decision about the most likely explanation, is there anything it might be important for you to try to notice next time? If so, how might you set yourself to do that?]"

Using the model in different situations: variations of context

As always, different contexts (see Chapter 1) will make a difference in how the process of using the model unfolds. Some typical contexts in which the process does invariably differ from that described above are discussed below. I start with the 'time' dimension ('when' in the context of the developing mentor–mentee relationship).

First mentorial

The mentor explains what she/he will and will not do in these post-lesson mentorials and why. Also see 'First meetings', Chapter 2). This is particularly important in situations where the context expects, even requires, the mentor to have observed the lesson under discussion (see Chapter 7), and/or where it is expected that a mentor will 'provide feedback.'

For example, the mentor might say something like the following:

When we are discussing a lesson you have taught, my main aim will be to help you arrive at your own informed judgements on your work and decisions about what you want or need to do next. I have a five-step process in mind, which is based on how teachers learn, and I will guide you through this. You can ask me for ideas, if you want, at various points in this process, but you will do most of the talking. If all goes well and we can learn to use this way of working together, you will be satisfied when we finish our discussion and have concrete ideas to take away and work on. I don't need to have observed your lesson, I am not an assessor or inspector. Anyway, the important thing is what you notice – if 'a teacher's responsibility is his/her response-ability' then developing that depends in part on your ability to notice the feedback your pupils are giving you all the time so that you have something to 'respond' to! I know that's not easy when there are so many other things on your mind. Anyway, that's how this process starts. In the first step, I ask you to think back to the lesson and describe part of it to me so that I can see and hear it as you did, and we go on from there. So, shall we have a try?

Early mentorials

Mentees face two main challenges with Step 1 in early post-lesson mentorials. The first relates to finding their focus, and the second to avoiding interpretations and judgements and staying with descriptions. Mentors therefore have to work hard initially in order to ensure that all mentorials 'start right.'

Finding the focus

Beginning mentees typically start Step 1 with an overview description of a lesson. This (particularly with beginning teachers) may amount to little more than a description of the plan and a list of what the mentee did. Even in these cases, where what the mentee actually describes is limited, most often a mentor will be able to hear or see some signs of mentee pleasure or displeasure during the account. This might indicate that a mentee would be ready to work on understanding the causes (or validity) of those feelings in order to be able to either plan to do things in similar ways in future, to gain more positive feelings or to plan to do things differently to get fewer negative feelings. A mentor can try saying something like:

When you talked about that part of the lesson you seemed pleased. You could choose to make that part of the lesson a focus for our discussion today, and then you might be better equipped to make more parts of future lessons go just as well. What do you think? Yes? Ok, so what exactly did you notice that prompted those feelings when you were remembering and telling me about it? Can you describe it in much greater detail? What exactly did you do and say, and what did the pupils do and say? Help me make a mental video!

Remaining descriptive

In normal life we all make and act upon immediate interpretations and judgements - no one would ever be able to cross a road, for example, if we didn't. In the time it would take us to consciously work out speeds of oncoming traffic and calculate the speed needed for walking across the road and avoiding that traffic, the moment would pass, the opportunity for crossing would have gone. So too in the classroom, in the midst of action, there is no time for a teacher to consciously recall, for example, the various theories or school policy in place for dealing with unwanted pupil behaviour. When pupils are, for example, engaged in some kind of shouting match, immediate action is called for. But the starting point for reflection, when there is time to consider things carefully, is different. Beginning teachers or mentees will typically offer up judgements, interpretations, generalisations and even solutions initially when asked to re-view in Step 1. Mentors often need to work hard to encourage the mentee to 'get back to' what she/he actually noticed that prompted the interpretations and judgements being offered and to suspend decisions and judgements until later in the process.

A typical early conversation goes something like this:

Mentee: Oh, dear, it was a boring lesson!

Mentor: Ok so that's your initial judgement, but what did you notice that makes you think that?

Mentee: Well, the pupils were bored.

Mentor: Mmm. That's one interpretation of something you noticed. What was it, can you remember?

Mentee: Well, there was this group of pupils who just sat there yawning.

Mentor: Ok. So some pupils yawned. How many in that group? Which pupils - tell me more about them. And the rest of the class, what were they doing?

[...]

Mentor: Ok, so I can see the scene. What seems to have concerned you was that three boys yawned during the X activity. Shall we make that the focus of our discussion today? (mentee nods) Ok, so let's move now to Step 2. You have already said that one possible interpretation is that they were bored. Before deciding on that, can you think of any other possible explanations or interpretations? Make as long a list as you can, and even include any ideas that may seem unlikely to you now.

Early challenges - general

One general early challenge for mentors is that some mentees will automatically assume that ideas you offer when invited are 'the right' ones. This can undermine your efforts to support the mentee in trusting their own informed judgements and decisions. To try to avoid this, mentors have, when invited:

- offered whacky, implausible ideas in Step 2 – ones which demonstrate how to 'think different things' and that are in fact unlikely to be chosen at Step 4;
- wondered aloud whether such and such a theory might be helpful to the discussion at step 3 or sounded doubtful about the utility and/or relevance or claimed to be unable to see the usefulness at the moment;
- modelled a 'light-bulb' moment at Step 3 (for example, "I know, doesn't Csikszentmihalyi's idea about 'flow' have something to say about boredom?") (see Chapter 8); or
- made sure, where they could, to always offer – when invited to do so – more than one idea/option for 'what to do next' at Step 5.

A second general early challenge for *mentors* can be coping with a mentee arriving at decisions that you suspect are less helpful than the ones you might have chosen. The temptation to intervene can be huge. However, if, by the end of Step 5, the mentee is ready to notice whether or not what they have chosen to try actually works, you need not worry. The mentee is learning – and all learners (need to) make mistakes or be less than perfect. (And see 'what ifs' below).

A last common general challenge for mentors is learning to 'trust the process.' Mentors can feel somewhat panicked if the mentee chooses a focus and the mentor, mentally jumping ahead, cannot immediately see any Step 5 outcomes. (Perhaps these feelings spill over from roles where we do have to 'know' and then tell people, which is not the case here.) When I and my mentor colleagues have felt like this and when we have trusted the process and just guided the mentee step by step, it has, without exception, resulted in the mentee finding practical ways forward for themselves and their pupils. Over time, we learn to be curious and excited rather than panicked, and make ourselves, as well as the mentee, take things step by step.

Early challenges in each step (2 to 5)

While Step 1 can be the most challenging to support initially (see above and 'Rationale: On Noticing', below), the other steps also have their challenges.

Step 2

The challenge for a mentor here is to wait for the mentee to think up more and more possible (even if seemingly implausible) interpretations. This requires us as mentors above all to have patience and trust – trust that the mentee can and will think of more possible interpretations, if given time. It can be quite a silent time as the mentee thinks, and this may not initially feel very comfortable to mentors – especially when, in busy teaching lives, 'getting on' and 'just doing it' may be the norm, or when you have ideas that you want to share but have not (perhaps only 'yet') been invited to do so. Mentors sometimes busy themselves keeping a list of the ideas the mentee generates (with the mentee's agreement) to try to avoid the temptation to fill the silences. This list can also be really useful later to compensate for less-than-excellent memories.

Step 3

At this step, you are inviting the mentee to recall what they have learnt or are learning that might be useful to the discussion. In some contexts, where the mentee is still a student teacher, for example, and where you have seen the college or university curriculum they are following, it may be quite easy for you to ask: "Umm, perhaps you have learnt something about 'boredom' and 'keeping pupils' interest' in your methodology class or in that module called 'learning'?" This could help your mentee remember some useful ideas.

However, it may be more difficult for your mentee to remember ideas she/he was once taught or heard about if that was some time ago and they were ideas the mentee dismissed as 'just theory' and never learnt to use. If you can, and if invited, do share stories of how you used such and such a theory/idea in a similar situation to help you understand the issue and decide on a plan of action – but don't worry if you can't.

Mentors, especially in early mentorials, can find themselves 'stuck' at this step, and in this case choose either to:

- work only from what the mentee knows about the context and the specific pupils and class, and make 'finding out what others say/write about the topic' a learning point at step 5, or
- 'pause' the mentorial and make agreements to survey people, books or articles to find out more about the topics raised before another meeting to continue the process at a next meeting within a day or two (part 2 of the mentorial).

Mentors find it reassuring that they do not have to know about everything the mentee knows or is being taught – they just need to know how to help the mentee remember this and use it in their 'workings out.'

Step 4

The challenge here is to help the mentee make a convincing argument and have 'robust reasoning' (Johnson, 1999). In other words, the mentee will ideally have more than one 'reason' (a contextual one and a theoretical one, for example) for their choice of interpretation or explanation and reasons why the other ideas on the 'possible list' are unlikely.

Step 5

Ensuring the full process is completed within the time available while still allowing ample thinking time can be a challenge, especially in early mentorials. It is important that the mentee completes Step 5, too, and so leaves the mentorial satisfied that she/he has been guided to make his/her own decisions and has concrete and specific things to do to progress his/her own learning and that of his/her own pupils.

In contexts with explicit standards for the mentee's teaching – periodic review

In many/most contexts, mentees are or will be expected to provide evidence or demonstrate that their teaching meets contextual standards at the end of their programmes or at some point(s) in their careers. In such cases, periodically asking the mentee to think back over a number of post-lesson mentorials and match evidence (noticing data) against the standards can be a helpful exercise (and see Chapters 1 and 7). This can usefully be conducted after a normal five-step post-lesson mentorial when the mentor can join the mentee in remembering instances that could be categorised as evidence of one standard or another.

Rationale behind the five-steps model

The development of the model

Mentors need to avoid judgementoring (see Introduction) and not 'provide feedback', but they do need *something* to do in a post-lesson context. This 'something' needs to replace the more well-known practices associated with assessment and judgementoring – however 'constructive' or 'supportive' they are thought to be. (One such is 'the feedback sandwich' in which criticism is 'sandwiched' between two slices of praise; that is, an observer offers judgements on 'what went well', then on 'what to improve', and ends with further 'what went well' praise.)

As mentoring is about supporting teacher learning, teachers say they learn best from experience, and learning is what the mentee needs to (learn to) do. It is this teacher learning process that needed to be conceptualised and then, in a scaffolding move, 'broken into steps' (see Introduction for a bit more on these ideas). This focus on a view of the teacher learning process was how the model above was developed. Three further terms were also central. The first two were at the foreground of my thinking, and the third was one of a cluster of ideas that have underpinned my practice for decades. They are 'feedback', 'noticing' and 'reflective practice' which I briefly discuss below.

On feedback

The meaning of the word 'feedback' has changed over time. Its origins are in electronics and, as I understand it, describe the response sent back to the originator of some action – the squeals coming out of the speakers when the electric guitarist gets too close them are, I think, an example. Nowadays, in education, the meaning of the term has changed, and 'feedback' is used euphemistically to describe the judgements given by someone who was *not* the original receiver of the action. An observer of a lesson who 'provides feedback' to the teacher was not a receiver of the teaching, he/she was not one of the learners. In my view, they are providing their judgements based on what they noticed, which will inevitably be limited (see below). The most valuable form of feedback, in its original sense, is provided by the learners in any class. Everything the learners do and say in response to what the teacher does and says is feedback. It is also invaluable feedback when and if the teacher notices it and uses it as the starting point for their systematic informed reflections.

On Noticing

First, let me explain what I mean by Noticing and how this overlaps with observation, following the distinction made by Mason (2002). I will then set out the reason why Noticing is so important to teachers, and why and how in more detail a mentor can support a mentee to notice more. By 'noticing' I mean what strikes you, what you pay attention to. 'Observing' is purposeful and often carried out by someone outside the action. An observer sets out to *try* to notice things, which they may or may not have specified in advance, and which they may or may not, in fact, notice. Even though you are more likely to notice those things you do specify beforehand, it does not mean you will.

If mentees have not noticed things during lessons, they cannot re-view them (see them again), and their reflection may be less useful (see below). If teachers do not notice the feedback pupils give them all the time, they cannot be responsive teachers and cater to their pupils' learning needs. If teaching means 'supporting pupils' learning', teachers' abilities to notice are key. You might be wondering why this should be a problem – after all, we all have eyes and ears and do notice things. But you may also have realised that different people notice different things – and not just because we may have viewed the same event from different physical angles.

Mason (2002) gives three possible scenarios when discussing noticing and perception which are really useful for mentors. The first scenario, the strongest noticing, is one in which we 'mark' something and can and do 're-mark' on it or talk about it. So, what or who a mentee talks about initially in Step 1 tells us as mentors what a mentee already marks, that is, has easily noticed, and therefore what is or was the most meaningful to them. I call this type of Noticing 'mark-Noticing.'

The second scenario is one in which something available for Noticing does register somewhere but is not 'marked' and so not volunteered in descriptions. However, if asked about it specifically, the Noticer can recall it and talk about it. So, in situations where the mentee initially talks in terms of 'I did this, then I did that', a mentor might ask, for example, "Ok, I can see what you were doing then, but I don't have a clear picture of how pupils in your class were responding." If the mentee can describe this, then their noticing of learner feedback was in Mason's second scenario. When mentees learn that you will be asking them for more and more detail, their attention can expand to include the kinds of things you ask about and their mark-Noticing develop. In my experience, there is almost always more a mentor can ask to encourage mentees to learn to mark more and therefore have more available to review when reflecting alone.

For example, the 'normal' or 'familiar' is easy to ignore. In normal life, this is sensible as it helps us avoid expending unnecessary effort and save noticing brainpower for more important things. On the other hand, it might be vitally important in life to notice unfamiliar, unwanted or unexpected things (for example, a lion about to pounce!) and perhaps, because of this, they are easier to notice, if tiring. Noticing beyond the 'easy' requires even more effort. Just think how tired you get using lots of brainpower when trying to navigate around an unfamiliar place. So, it is natural for teachers to find the unexpected, unwanted or unusual behaviour of pupils easy to mark, even though explanations and solutions may be found in the behaviour of other classmates.

A mentor engaged in genuinely trying to make a mental video of the class might ask, for example, "Ok, I can see in my mental video what those boys were doing, but I can't see the rest of the class. What were they doing, how did they respond, what did they do or say?" Assuming the noticing was in scenario two and available for recall, this might prompt that mentee to start mark-Noticing pupils 'behaving' and start giving attention to quiet diligent pupils, to girls as well as boys, and thus even reduce unwanted behaviour (through a 'catching them doing it right' approach). So, the key for mentors listening to mentee descriptions of the agreed-upon focus in Step 1 is to work hard on making a clear picture for *themselves* – asking the questions they need answered in order to do so. These may include questions about the physical setting. Even when you and your mentee both work in the same school, wall displays may change, for example, or a particular room may be noisier or warmer than another, and this may have a bearing on the issue. Some mentors find it helpful to think of themselves in Step 1 as a film director, gathering details in order to be able to recreate the scene in a new film.

There is a third scenario, one in which one person can Notice something but for another it just doesn't register at all, and if you ask them about it, they cannot tell you. What makes the difference here (apart from physical sight lines, for example) might be what the two potential noticers know *about*. For example, I know nothing about the discipline of ice dancing. I can watch two couples perform and just think both performances were beautiful. The Olympic judges, however, give the couples very different marks. I just did not notice any differences as from my perspective – they both twirled, did lifts and stayed upright. I *would* have noticed an unexpected and unwanted fall. So, it is true that mentors who probably know more *about* teaching than their mentees are more likely to notice more if they observed the mentee's class than the mentee themselves. However, mentors are different from assessors (see Introduction and Chapter 7), and what matters in learning teaching is what the *mentee* notices, every day, for themselves in their own classes, rather than what some occasional outside observer might notice. In addition, what any outside observers actually notice says as much if not more about the observer (what's in their heads, what they value and so on) than about the teacher they are observing. From the perspective of this third scenario, the more a mentee knows *about* teaching in ways that are relevant to them and their classes, the more potentially they *can* notice, and this is another valuable aspect of Step 3.

The need to develop a mentee's skills in noticing through eliciting the mentee's descriptions of moments in past lessons – what they had mark-Noticed – was the main reason for the realisation that *mentors* (as opposed to trainers – see Introduction and Chapter 4) could work in a more genuine and authentic way if they had *not* observed the class. Otherwise, if you had been there, a mentee could reasonably wonder why you needed to ask them to describe what happened.

On reflective practice

Before developing this protocol, I knew from my reading (including Donald Schon's seminal works in the 1980s (Schon, 1983, 1987) and others since – though I still have not gone back to what many argue are the origins of the term in Dewy's 1933 text – that being a reflective practitioner and helping others become reflective practitioners was a key aspect of professional learning programmes. I had puzzled over various descriptions of reflective cycles and wondered what the labels meant I should actually *do* as a teacher and then as a ToT. Kolb's labels (1984) 'do, review, learn, apply' gave me the starting points for several avenues of exploration. In particular, thinking about the 'review' – or 're-view', seeing again – phase led to 'noticing' (see above). 'Learn' is such an easy short word, but it led to years of work (see Malderez and Wedell, 2007). And I questioned altogether the place of the word/metaphor 'apply' in education. Like 'deliver', 'apply' is not a dead metaphor. We still apply plasters to wounds and paint to walls to cover up flaws or faults. In education, we need to *use* ideas/outcomes of our learning rather than 'apply' them and stick them on top for show. Rather than cover up, we need to uncover our own and our pupils' thoughts and feelings in order to address them appropriately and support learning.

These days, policy documents and programme aims around the world – from China to Chile and England to Ethiopia – now include the term 'reflective practitioner', although how this is achieved is often less evident. In some contexts, I am not sure it is actually desired, at least as I understand the term (see Chapter 4) – that is, not every country actually wants teachers to be autonomous professionals making their own decisions. However, I also knew from experience and research (Bardhun, 1998) that we couldn't assume that people would start programmes already knowing how to engage in reflective practice. Reflective practice needed to have a specific focus in the teacher learning curriculum, and such practice needed to occur *after* a mentee's experiences of teaching, which, by definition, is about learning from and for professional experiences.

However, I first developed the protocol as a result of realising that what mattered was a *mentee's* noticing, recognising that 'observation and providing feedback' were not very supportive *mentor* activities and after having reconsidered teacher knowledge and the processes for learning it (see Introduction, Malderez and Wedell, 2007). In other words, I set out to find a practical, non-judgemental replacement for 'providing constructive feedback' which would support teachers in developing their noticing and Know To skills. I also needed a way for those teachers to, in a baking metaphor, 'fold' theory 'into' their developing IKB, so that they learn to see its practical relevance. It was only *after* I had developed the protocol that I saw that it could also be viewed as a way to coach the reflective practice skills of teachers in a systematic and informed way. I also decided that, for me, reflective practice, rather than being cyclical, is u-shaped, like the arc of a swinging pendulum. It is the momentum that builds up from the movement to and fro that moves the pendulum along the horizontal zip wire of progress and development.

Enough! Let's get back to more practical issues now and look at some typical reservations that mentors I have worked with have had.

'Yes, buts…' and 'what ifs…'

Mentors (-to-be) have questioned many things about this type of post-lesson mentorial when first introduced to it and before using the five-step model. Some of these yes, buts… and what ifs… are set out in the table below, with the kind of responses from others in the training group that were usually given. One of the questioners gave a presentation at a conference in Nepal some years later entitled 'The miracle of the 5 steps', which suggests the responses must have been reassuring and convincing enough – for that mentor anyway, not only to try it, but to make it a valuable experience for both the mentee and the mentor.

Table 6.2 Reservations and responses

Yes, buts…and what ifs…	Responses
Yes, but my mentee seems to have so many problems, and you are asking me to spend a whole hour on just one. Wouldn't it be quicker for me to observe and then just tell her?	Yes, it would be quicker, but so much less effective (as well as potentially bringing the dangers of judgementoring). Why less effective? Four reasons: a) Because the mentee may or may not be 'ready' to learn what the mentor chooses; b) the mentee is not left with ideas for *how* to learn/change things: c) the mentee cannot learn how to learn, *And*, d) the mentee can also learn in ways that 'solve' the problems we may identify by choosing 'what went well' as a focus. At a time when they are vulnerable learners and need confidence-boosting, this may be the best option for the focus – it's not just about 'problems.' Deep transformative learning takes time – as does effective mentoring.
Yes, but I am *required* to observe and provide constructive feedback.	Yes, some documentation does use the words 'observe and provide constructive feedback.' But when we look at *why* we are asked to do this, it is because the writers want us to support learning (see Introduction/Chapter 1). If we do this in a more effective way, surely, in most contexts, no one will blame us. If we are required to 'do observations', we may be able to choose when these occur and use them productively – and/but not as a basis for subsequently 'providing feedback/our judgements' (and see Chapter 7).
Yes, but my mentee *wants* me to help her, to tell her what to do.	Many beginning teachers believe (still) that there is one right way of teaching and that 'someone' (the mentor) knows what it is and should tell them. They also seem to believe that once we have told them, or shown them, this will somehow mean they can do it. It doesn't. When mentees are like this, it may tell us that our mentee is at the start of their learning teaching journey, and part of our work is to help them (in a pedagogical way, that is, scaffold – see Introduction) see that they have to develop their own best way of teaching, that there is no one 'best way.' And we have plenty of opportunities to share what we know (particularly in steps 3 and 5) and at times in our other roles.

(Continued)

(Continued)

Yes, buts...and what ifs...	Responses
What if, in the description of the lesson, I hear something that obviously needs addressing urgently, but she/he doesn't choose it as the focus?	Our mentees can't learn everything at once, and we might find ways (see section Other possible activities in the Educator role) of getting the mentee to mark-Notice the issue that concerns us.
	Very, very rarely, we may hear about (or notice in an observation) something that really does seem to us to need urgent attention. I am thinking of a description of corporal punishment I once heard about where it was not illegal in that educational context at the time (see anecdote in Chapter 4). In this case, I did suggest in Step 1 that this should be the focus for the discussion that day. That discussion eventually led the mentee to muse on the possibility that powerful adults beating children might contribute to those children, when grown up, 'instinctively' choosing violence as the way to resolve conflict. The mentee prepared a different strategy to try when faced with 'misbehaviour.'
	So, I would be a hypocrite if I said 'always' leave the mentee to choose the focus! As always, context is everything.
	It might be helpful to decide before the mentoring begins what your personal and any legal or disciplinary 'red lines' are. These will usually relate to teacher behaviour that might put pupils in physical or psychological danger. You then only intervene at step 1 if those lines seem to have been crossed. In most cases, this will never be necessary.

2. Pre-lesson mentorial

Aims

- To support the mentee in preparing to teach a lesson (the 'preparation of self' phase of lesson preparation - see 'Rationale' below).
- To train the mentee in a way of thinking and of imagining and picturing the future lesson in a way which should enable them to achieve (most of) their aims whatever, in fact, happens.
- To support the development of more effective lesson-planning.
- To leave the mentee with a sense of confidence and preparedness.

Materials

Mentee-prepared lesson plan. Handout of (first two columns of) the table below.

Timing

Before a lesson, when a lesson plan has been developed and 'concrete preparation' (for example, of extra materials a teacher needs to take to class) is underway, but when there is enough time for any minor adjustments to be made (for example, a day before the lesson)

Time needed

15 to 45 minutes

Procedure

The mentor prompts the mentee to think aloud and find different types of answers to the questions about the lesson plan in the table below.

Table 6.3 Helping mentees prepare to teach

Question	Focus	Possible mentor prompts
		Ok, so let's think this through and get you ready!
What	The aims of the teaching	So, what do you want the students to learn in this lesson?
Why 1	Reason in terms of context (for example, curriculum, exam)	How are your aims related to our context, (coursebook, curriculum, exam)?
Why 2	Reason in terms of subject learning	Thinking about disciplinary learning, why might learning this help the pupils become better (language users/scientists/mathematicians, for example)
Why 3	Reason in terms of actual pupils/class	And what about your pupils? How does learning this connect to what they already know and can do?
How 1	How each activity and sequences of activities can support learning	What have you planned for your pupils to do so that they can learn what you want them to? How does each activity prepare them for the next?

(Continued)

(Continued)

Question	Focus	Possible mentor prompts
How 2	How the mentee mediates between the tasks and the learners – for example, what they will say, where they will stand and classroom management	For example: How will you introduce/give a pupil-focused purpose for this activity? (Might your answer to Why 3 above help you with this?) How will you give the instructions for this activity – how will you get attention, what will you say, how will you check all have understood, how will you monitor, how will you stop the activity, what will you do and say after and why?
What if (X?)	Imagining many examples of how the reality might differ from the plan, and what the mentee might do if this were the case; drawing on learning from post-lesson mentorials	How many 'what ifs' have you considered? Remembering our post-lesson discussions, what other 'what if' questions might it be useful to consider? What will you do 'if' – what contingency plans do you have in place? (For example, if pupils need more time to complete that activity/learning, how will you adjust your plan?) How will you know if you need to use your contingency plans? What might you notice to help you make that decision? Given our discussion, are there any tweaks you want to make to your plan? Where and why? Is there anything else you still want to do to prepare for the lesson? (For example, do you want/need to rehearse that story/those instructions?) Is there any other way I can help you feel prepared?

Variations of context

When time is limited

By 'limited' I mean when there is not enough time for a full pre-lesson mentorial, or when there is not enough time before the lesson to make (m)any changes to the plan itself. In these situations, and as the written plan provides information about 'What' and 'How 1', the main focus can be on 'How 2' and 'What if.' However, you may need to elicit the mentee's responses to 'Why' to support his/her thinking when considering 'how' if it seems to you that these are not being used in the mentee's reasoning.

Rationale for the pre-lesson mentorial protocol

Getting ready for a lesson has three stages.

Stage 1: Planning. Ideally, this stage involves a) deciding or understanding what the pupils will be expected to learn and why, and b) what activities/ processes they will be asked to engage in, in order to do so. I write 'ideally' because, although 'planning' usually results in some sort of written plan (from notes on a coursebook to a completed, contextually required pro-forma), it can involve only a list of activities in a notebook (a version of b).

Stage 2: Concrete preparation. This stage involves getting physical things ready, for example, visual aids, worksheets or equipment needed for the lesson and booking or making an appropriate (classroom) environment if necessary.

Stage 3: Preparation of self. This stage includes, for example, reminding oneself of the purposes, thinking through what to do and say at each stage and rehearsing, as necessary.

The first two stages (can) produce visible 'products', while the third equally – if not more – important phase does not. This results in two problems. The first is that the mentee will never have been exposed to 'models' of this 'preparation of self' phase and cannot easily understand its necessity/utility without pre-lesson mentorials of the type described above. Secondly, from the point of view of mentors, it is too easy to think that someone is ready to teach a lesson if an acceptable written plan and any materials needed to execute that plan are in evidence. However, the success of any lesson can depend on the thinking (as well as skills) of the person using that plan and materials. This is why it is so important that opportunities for learning this 'preparation of self' phase of lesson are provided – perhaps especially when the mentee is beginning to learn teaching skills.

I accept that many required lesson-plan formats are, in fact, tools to try to ensure that mentees do think appropriately about the forthcoming lessons. However, apart from the fact that different contexts have different formats to be filled in, and in many this is only required during the training process pre-qualification, the reality is that completing the plan can become a form-filling exercise. Regular pre-lesson mentorials of the type described above can also help 'planning' become a more meaningful process.

3. Mentorial record sheet completion

Aims

- To create evidence to provide to managers of mentoring schemes.
- To create useful reminders for mentees and mentors to use between mentorials.

Materials

Copies (hard or electronic) for both mentor and mentee of a mentorial record sheet.

Timing

After each mentorial

Time

3 to 5 minutes

Procedure

The mentee uses two or three minutes at the end of each mentorial to complete this sheet, with the mentor's help as needed.

   The mentee records only one or two main points in sections 1 to 3 to summarise the main focus and outcomes of the mentorial.

Mentorial Record Sheet No. ___

Mentee Name:
Mentor Name:
About this mentorial:
Date: _____Place:_____Time:_____Duration:_____
Topics discussed:

Mentee's conclusions/decisions:

Agreements made:
By mentee:
By mentor:

Signed: _____ & _____
(plus date if different from above for any reason)

Rationale for the use of a mentorial record sheet

Managers of mentoring schemes may need to evaluate their schemes and be sure, for example, that mentoring is in fact taking place. This is hard to do without visible evidence, of which there can be little, especially when mentors are in a context where they can choose not to observe mentee-taught lessons. In some contexts, it became clear there was a need to develop some kind of evidence to fulfil this need.

We wanted something that, ideally, would not breach confidentiality (in a threatening way at least), be quick and easy to make and be of practical use to all concerned: managers, mentors and mentees alike.

The mentee-completed form above need not reveal more than the general topics of conversation (for example, classroom management) and a brief decision (for example, use X technique next time). While a reader/manager can find value in knowing the general area that became a focus of the conversation, there is no way of knowing whether, for that particular mentee, these conclusions were reached as a result of something going well in a class or of a difficulty encountered. In this way, confidentiality is largely protected. Both mentor and mentee can use their copies of the mentorial record sheet as reminders: a mentor might have agreed/offered, for example, to look for a relevant book to lend, and a mentee might have agreed/decided to ask a few colleagues about something. These agreements would be easy to forget in the middle of a busy week of teaching. When both mentor and mentee get into the habit of glancing at the last mentorial record sheet a day or two before the next mentorial, they are more likely to fulfil agreements in time, and the mentoring process is supported.

4. Other possible activities in the Educator role

I list below just some of the activities any one mentee might choose to engage in to support their further learning. These are activities mentors may have suggested if asked during Step 5 discussions and/or helped organise for the mentee. Which, when or if such activities are in fact organised depends largely on the mentee's decisions and choices in Step 5 of post-lesson discussions. However, another source of inspiration a mentor can use when organising the details (for example, which teacher or class might be the most useful for the mentee to observe or talk to) might also be related to Step 1 and noticing skills development. For example, if your mentee is learning to notice more subtle signs of pupil learning or feelings, it might be helpful to suggest to the teacher that your mentee is planning to observe for other reasons that the mentee sit with a group of pupils in order to get the pupil perspective.

Other possible mentee activities include, for example:

- observing other teachers who have the skills the mentee has identified as wanting to learn;

- 'surveying' other members of staff;
- shadowing one or more pupils throughout a whole school day;
- attending a professional conference or training event with a particular learning goal in mind;
- collecting (from books, the internet or colleagues) at least three different 'classroom activities' for pupils with the same stated learning aims – to increase options in planning or when considering various 'what ifs' in lesson preparation; and/or
- keeping a noticing journal (that is, writing a short/one-page description [only] of a moment from the same lesson each week for a number of weeks and then comparing what was and what was not noticed [marked] each time and considering the possible effects of this, and/or comparing their journal entries with those of others).

I turn now to a chapter about assessing teaching. I have included this mainly for those mentors who are still required to add an assessor duties to those of a mentor. However, most of us will need to deal with the after-effects of others' assessments of our mentee at some point, and all of us need to advocate for more mentoring-friendly contexts. So do read on.

References

Bardhun, S. (1998), *Traits and conditions that accelerate teacher learning*. Unpublished doctoral dissertation. London: Thames Valley University.

Claxton, G. (2004), Learning is learnable (and we ought to teach it). In J. Cassell (Ed.) *Ten years on*. Bristol: National Commission for Education.

Johnson, K. (1999), *Understanding language teaching: reasoning in action*. Boston: Heinle and Heinle.

Kolb, D.A. (1984), *Experiential learning: experience as the source of learning and development*. Englewood Cliffs, NJ: Prentice Hall.

Malderez, A. & Wedell, M. (2007), *Teaching teachers: processes and practices*. London: Continuum.

Mason, J. (2002), *Researching your own practice: the discipline of noticing*. London: Routledge.

Schön, D. (1983), *The reflective practitioner: how professionals think in action*. New York: Basic Books.

Schön, D. (1987), *Educating the reflective practitioner: towards a new design for teaching and learning in the professions*. San Francisco, CA: Jossey-Bass.

7 Dealing with assessing your mentees (and with others' assessments of them)

Introduction

This chapter is about the formal assessments your mentee may have to undergo, particularly when you are their assessor. It describes what you as their mentor can do to help your mentees prepare for, make the most of, and minimise any negative after-effects of such assessments. You will have encountered some of these ideas already in Chapters 2, 3 and 6 particularly.

However, acting also as a formal assessor is something (I fear still many) 'unlucky' readers may have to undertake in addition to many other duties as a mentor, and this chapter is, in the immediate practical sense, perhaps mainly for you. One of the reviewers of my book proposal suggested that the use of the term 'unlucky' might be off-putting to some readers. This is far from my intention, so why *do* I say 'unlucky readers'? I chose this way of describing mentor-assessors in part because of the additional challenges it poses to effective mentoring (the N for non-evaluative in ONSIDE, see Introduction), which I describe throughout this chapter, but also because it doesn't need to be this way. I remember a moment talking to a case study participant in research I was involved in who talked about being 'lucky' with the mentor she had and thinking at the time that effective mentoring shouldn't be a matter of luck. That thought led to redoubled efforts in providing mentor development opportunities, including to my writing this book. I hope that talking about mentor-assessors as being 'unlucky' may prompt similar thoughts and actions in those ToT readers who can and do influence programme design.

So, are you one of the unlucky ones? You are (or were) if, when you engaged in the exploration of your context proposed in Chapter 1, you identified the requirement to formally assess your mentee. I hope you now see this as an indicator that your context does not (yet) fully support ONSIDE mentoring (see Introduction). Some of you may have been able to act on the outcomes of that exploration and shift the main burden of such assessment elsewhere (for example, to someone in the accrediting body or someone in the managerial hierarchy in the school). If you have, that's great and should make things easier for you. It

DOI: 10.4324/9781003429005-8

means you are not now in this group. Others – the 'unlucky' ones – may still have assessor duties. Having to combine roles can make your job as a mentor so much more *difficult* although I hope the practical ideas in the 'What mentors do: for "unlucky" readers' section below will help. You may have realised some of these difficulties while working through other chapters in this book. As well as making things more difficult for a mentor, adding the duties of an assessor to all the others being a mentor entails just adds to your, probably already overburdened, workload. Perhaps this is one of the reasons why many so-called mentors who are also tasked with the formal assessor role seem to focus only or mainly on assessing. This is understandable if they are in contexts where:

- assessment reports are the only expected visible products of their work;
- their own experience is one of only ever having been assessed and never truly mentored;
- they have had no, insufficient or inappropriate preparation for their roles as a mentor, so they don't know or have the skills for any other way to act or to be; and
- they have not been given sufficient *time* to mentor or to prepare to mentor and develop as a mentor.

Whatever your situation, it is likely that all of you will need to support your mentee through assessment processes in your mentor role, whether you are directly involved in the assessment itself or not. What's more, you 'lucky' ones may one day change contexts and find yourselves needing arguments to avoid or find ways to deal with combining mentoring with the requirements of conducting formal assessments. Finally, all teacher mentors, whatever the context, will ideally be coming together to advocate for mentoring-friendly contexts (see Introduction, Chapter 8 and Conclusions). So, really, I am writing this chapter for all of you, even if not all of you will need to use all of the practical ideas described.

There are four main parts to this chapter. I start with some of my own stories of being assessed, before inviting you to recall your own experiences. Going back to reflect on our own personal-professional histories can help us understand our own starting viewpoints and prepare us to challenge those aspects we have taken for granted. Next, I write about the need for assessors and assessing teachers more generally. I then compare assessors and mentors in terms of what they do and don't do and how combining these roles challenges effective mentoring. The final part, 'What mentors do', is divided into two sections. I first address those readers who are still required to add being an assessor to their mentor roles and describe how mentors have handled the challenges in ways that might minimise the negative impact on their mentoring.

Being observed and assessed

My stories

Many decades ago and before there were formal school-based mentors involved at any time in a teacher's career, I was a student teacher and did my first 'teaching practice' (as it was called then) in a secondary modern school in England. A tutor came out from the university-based programme to observe a lesson and assess my efforts. We had to 'pass' a certain number of observed and assessed lessons in order to 'pass' this aspect of the programme. Recently, I came across a poem entitled The Day the Tutor Came that I wrote after one such visit. Now, I do remember the occasion and how it made me feel, and I can still 'see' the classroom and some of the pupils, but I had forgotten some of the details I found in the poem. I won't bore you with the whole thing, mainly because it isn't very good (!), but I will use a few extracts as I tell the story of this experience. The lesson started well. I write about "strolling" into the classroom and of being "happy to hear the hubbub of excitement" as I explained the lesson and set the first task. My assessor sat in the corner scribbling. Things went downhill from there. I write about "not recognising the menacing sounds of disorder" and of losing control, until, somewhat in desperation no doubt, I "issue paper and topic to write about." My assessor got up and left – the room and the premises. There was no point in him staying as I had abandoned my plan. Even going off plan slightly was a reason to "fail" the assessment. The pupils were clearly shocked to see the tutor leave. I record "their sorrowing faces" and the question a pupil asks me: "Miss, did you pass the test, miss?" The poem ends by describing my feelings of worthlessness, as I had not only failed the assessment but let my pupils down, too. It concludes "and so I failed twice the day the tutor came."

I know I seriously considered dropping out of the programme, but I didn't. Over time, having eventually 'passed' and qualified, I developed more expertise and confidence. I was eventually confident enough to shrug off a negative assessment I felt indignant about. This time I was criticised because I "let the students make a mistake", which was a cardinal sin for language teachers at the time because of a prevailing behaviourist view of language learning. I had responded to signs of boredom from my students after an hour of controlled, mistake-free language lab drills and set up an activity where they could use the language (rather than just practise) and talk about what was meaningful to them. However, this time I refused to feel bad just because I had responded to signs of boredom or wanted to give them practice in using the language.

In fact, most subsequent assessments left me in states of indignation. I recall, for example, being told by an assessor from the Inspectorate of the system I was working in that I should have made the aims of the lesson clear to the learners. In my view, I *had* given them reasons and purposes for what was to come. Perhaps my assessor just had not noticed it, or he expected me to state *my* lesson aims or hoped-for 'learning outcomes' (see 'Whys' in pre-lesson mentorial, Chapter 6). I had learnt from reflections on my experiences that telling learners what you hoped they'd learn in the lesson at the start then asking at the end what they *had* in fact learnt would inevitably lead to echoes of what I had said at the start – and told me nothing. Much more engaging was telling my learners that I had planned the upcoming lesson in terms, perhaps, of difficulties they had had in the previous lesson, something I noticed last time or of one or more of the group goals we had agreed on at the start of our work together. For me, a *lesson* is not the highest unit of teaching. From a teacher's perspective, a *course* is. The *process* of learning, which differs from group to group in pace and often route, spans many lessons. Helping learners realise how a particular lesson fits into *their* process is what is important. But my assessor didn't give me the chance to explain this. I felt deskilled and that my professionalism was not valued, even when I understood the truism that in all educational assessments what is measured is what is measurable rather than what is valuable. I privately resolved to get better at displaying what my assessors wanted to see. I discovered many years later that this response was/is a common one. There are now many, many articles on this phenomenon, which has been attributed to 'performativity' cultures, 'datafication', overbearing inspection regimes leading to 'fabrication', individual inspector/assessor skills and so on (see, e.g., Macruaic and Harford, 2008; Hobson and McIntyre, 2013). To me, it is just being human! I am going to be judged by a powerful 'other' whose words will have an impact on me and my school. I have no ongoing relationship with the inspector, and she/he doesn't know me or my class as well as I do. For the sake of my school, if not my pupils, I will have to know very well what they might want to see and try to show them what they want in that one lesson.

It is clear that these experiences made me think about my teaching and question myself. It is equally clear to me as I relive these experiences, that I would not have chosen to go to those assessors for help with any teaching dilemmas. I think I did, however, go to the tutor in the first example, although I don't remember what was said. I explain that now as being in part because it was expected. I was also at the beginning of my learning teaching journey, and I expect that, like many such learners, I believed that he could tell me what was right and what to do, and that being told could somehow immediately transform me into someone who could 'do it right.' If it didn't, that was my fault, not his or the fault of the system.

Of course, things have changed since my first story. But, as I have noted earlier (see, for example, Chapters 1 and 8), our own past experiences are a huge influence not only on what feels right to us to do but on what we *will* do 'in extremis' or 'on the hoof' if we have not re-examined those influences and had enough time to practice any alternative strategies we have found or developed. Events in my own personal-professional story such as those recounted above have probably contributed to my passion for effective mentoring.

Your stories

Your turn. Ideally, take turns with a colleague to act as listener and speaker as you recall your experiences.

1.   Think back to one or more occasions when your teaching was observed and assessed. If you can, choose one occasion from very early on, when you were a student teacher perhaps, and another from when you were more experienced. Try to remember details about what happened and how you felt, what the assessment was and how you felt about that.
2.   Ask yourself:
     •   How would you now explain your reactions then? Is there anything in earlier chapters that might support your explanations?
     •   What does your own experience tell you about the assessment of observed lessons? How does this relate to how you now understand an effective mentoring process?

About assessors and assessing teaching

My view that you are 'unlucky readers' if you have to combine mentor and assessor duties might suggest that I think assessors are not valuable or needed in any system. This is not the case. There is a managerial and political argument for ensuring that people becoming teachers are at an acceptable standard and that standards are at least maintained or at best raised throughout our careers. At one time, and still in some contexts, many teacher assessments were solely pen and paper ones requiring displays of a teacher's knowledge *about* a subject (see Introduction). Later on, and reasonably, it was felt that what mattered as well as, or perhaps more than, what a teacher knew *about* was *how*, in practice, a teacher supported pupil learning. Lesson observations became the main tool for the data gathering on which such assessments were, and still are, made. (In some contexts, teacher-produced credential or development portfolios have been added to or replaced observation-based assessment; see, e.g., Hobson et al., 2010). It soon became clear that making assessments based on lesson observations is both time-consuming and expensive. Conflating mentor and assessor duties seemed, I think, reasonable as an (apparently) cost-saving move to many managers. Given that the prevailing thinking about teacher mentoring in many contexts seemed, and seems still, to centre on a belief that what mentors do is observe mentees teaching and then 'provide constructive feedback' (in what I would call a Trainer role – see Introduction, Chapters 1, 4 and 6) the argument must have gone something like this: "if mentors would be observing classes and making judgements anyway, and know the mentee and school better, why not conflate the roles and save time and money?" Many teacher mentors are still required to assess as well as mentor, using lesson observation as the main or only tool. This is true even in contexts where 'coaching', also a *non-judgemental* support process, is seen, in the rhetoric at least, as part of, or as an adjunct to, mentoring as they understand it (see Introduction, Chapter 1), and where the 'standards' a mentee must achieve cover more than in-class performance.

I first look more closely at what assessors of teaching using lesson observation do and how it relates to what mentors do, before describing processes mentors have devised which might minimise the potential problems if you are one of the 'unlucky ones.'

Comparing what assessors and mentors do

Assessors of teaching using lesson observation usually:

1. observe teachers teaching one or more lessons;
2. interpret what they happen to notice;
3. attempt to make judgements about the quality of the teaching against contextual standards (which may or may not be written and explicit in that context);
4. (in some contexts, discuss or communicate the assessment outcomes with the observed teachers, and) report those judgements to others who are in a more powerful position than the observed teacher.

In earlier chapters, I have set out the background, justification and detail about what mentors might do in relation to the four aspects listed above. Some of these are summarised in the table below. There are also clues earlier in the book about why being both a mentor and an assessor of observed lessons are in conflict. The impact this might have on the effectiveness of the mentoring process is also summarised in the table.

What mentors do

For 'unlucky' readers – mentors who must also assess

As Table 7.1 shows, your role as mentor fundamentally conflicts with the practices of an assessor. If you are in the situation where you are required to observe your mentee's teaching and report your assessments of that teaching to others, you will want to work out a way of doing this with as little negative impact on your mentoring as possible. What follows are descriptions of ways mentors I have worked with have devised and used.

Table 7.1 Assessors and mentors: comparisons and problems

	Assessor	Mentor	Risks when roles combined
(i) Observe	May or may not notice features of the visible aspects of teaching related to contextual standards on which to base an assessment.	Is centrally concerned with supporting the development of the mentee's own noticing skills, and for this does not need to observe classes. (Chapter 6; see also earlier chapters for reasons and situations when it might be appropriate.)	Mentees may believe that their mentor notices more (which is probably accurate) and continue to want to let the mentor 'do it (the noticing) for them', thus undermining learnacy development.
(ii) Interpret	May or may not consider a variety of possible interpretations of observed features or seek further information to help decide which is the most likely to be the case.	Is centrally concerned with supporting the mentee in generating a range of possible interpretations of noticed phenomena and of seeking further information and/or recalling information encountered elsewhere ('theory') which helps the mentee decide the most likely interpretation.	Again, mentees may believe that it is easier and quicker for the mentor to interpret for them, and learnacy development is further undermined. More importantly, perhaps, if mentees are relieved of the necessity of making the 'theory' they have encountered relevant and useful to them through this process of deciding on the most likely interpretation, they may 'get cut off' permanently from 'theory', and the development not only of their own IKB but also of the profession is compromised.

(Continued)

(Continued)

	Assessor	Mentor	Risks when roles combined
(iii) Judge	Draws conclusions and makes judgements based ostensibly on contextually accepted norms (but, inevitably, because of the nature of noticing, on personal norms, too).	Actively attempts to promote their mentees' ability to make their own informed judgements. To this end, actively attempts to withhold revealing their own judgements to a mentee – particularly vital but especially challenging when the mentee is a student teacher (see Chapter 6).	In the worst-case scenario, the mentee feels so patronised or attacked by the assessment outcomes that effective mentoring by that same person becomes impossible. Otherwise, as above, learnacy development is impeded.
(iv) Report	Reports on outcomes of assessments to, for example, Inspectorate, programme provider or line manager.	Safeguards the essential confidentiality of the mentoring relationship (see Chapter 2). (Mentors use the assessments of the mentee that they will inevitably *have*, to make their own private decisions about what to do next with or for their mentees.)	Again, breaching confidentiality can make the relationship feel unsafe to the mentee, and effective mentoring is then unlikely.

Understanding the criteria and your expectations (as assessor)

I discussed in Chapters 1, 2, 3 and 6, the need to support your mentee in understanding contextual standards, not only of being a teacher, but also of their teaching. This work is helpful not only with respect to a general role of helping mentees into the context/system, but also is an important part of your work in helping mentees prepare to be observed and assessed while teaching. I described understanding these standards as a main aim of a periodic review activity (see Chapter 6).

This same activity should also help your mentee understand what any assessor (you, in this case) might want or expect to, or in fact, notice in his or her teaching when having to make an assessment, and how this relates to contextually accepted standards.

As mentioned earlier, this familiarisation with the standards and what an assessor would need to notice need not involve you acting as an assessor or observing m/any lessons. Indeed, *not* observing lessons for as long as possible, I have argued, would help you in your mentoring work with your mentee, because:

- you might more easily avoid having insufficiently informed or inaccurate judgements (which, if revealed, could have disastrous effects on your mentoring work);
- your mentee is less likely, at the outset anyway, to ask for your judgements (just when you are working towards encouraging them to learn to make and trust their own);
- you would have a genuine reason for asking your mentee to describe what happened (and so support their development of noticing skills on which both KT and learnacy development depends); and
- you would save yourself timetabling issues and can use the time you would have spent in a mentee's classroom for more or longer mentorials.

So, there is nothing extra that mentors do here. Activities you are probably already engaging in for another purpose (understanding and integrating into the context) also serve to support your mentee in their preparations for assessment.

Supporting your mentee in getting comfortable with observers

Your mentee will ideally need to get as comfortable as possible with having someone in the classroom before the moment, or period, of any assessment which is based on or includes lesson observation. Why do I say that? I say it not just for the sake of your mentee's feelings (which, as discussed in earlier in for example, the Introduction and Chapter 2, are an important factor in teacher learning, indeed in any learning), but also because it affects the validity of the assessment. If teachers are not comfortable with the presence of observers in the classroom, their attention (which needs to be on the learners and potential signs of learning, or difficulties with it; see Chapter 6) will inevitably be on, or drawn to, the observers, which is likely to result in an atypical lesson, one which is less responsive to the learners than might otherwise be the case.

So, it matters:

- when you start observing classes;
- how you do so; and
- how you proceed in the post-observed-lesson mentorials.

When to start observing

Here is another time where context (from the regulations in your system and the context of school and its staff to your relationship with your mentee) is all important.

Ideally you would *not* want to observe your mentee teaching before:

- you have a good, trusting and long-standing relationship with your mentee;
- you judge that the mentee is now both willing and able to (and does) engage in systematic informed reflective practice alone; and
- the mentee actually asks you to do so.

However, if you are in a context where regular observations are required, practices effective mentors have used include:

- discussing the requirements regarding observed lessons and how you feel about these with your mentee at the start of the relationship;
- agreeing when any observations might begin, making this as far into the future as you feel able or your context allows, and making it clear that this date is still negotiable;
- before the first observed lesson, holding as many normal post-lesson mentorials as possible as well as at least one periodic review mentorial (so that you can discover later how this might change when what an observer has noticed is added to the evidence base on which judgements are made).
- Working hard during normal post-lesson mentorials to demonstrate or explain (see Chapter 6):
    - the importance of the mentees' noticing and the types of evidence you might be looking for (through your questioning and efforts to get a clear picture at Step 1, in post-lesson mentorials);
    - the fallibility of any observer's noticing, and
    - the validity of your mentee's own informed judgements (see Chapter 6).

How to conduct a required observation with your mentee

BEFORE

When nearing the agreed-upon date for the first observation, mentors have engaged in the following processes:

- Explaining what they will do during the observation. They will try to notice evidence to help them *both* later make judgements against the standards/criteria, and take notes on what they notice (see 'On noticing', Chapter 6, and below).
- Asking whether there is a particular standard or criterion the mentee is working on and would like them to try to get evidence for.
- Explaining how, after the observation, they propose to extend the normal post-lesson mentorial into a periodic review mentorial, this time considering the evidence they *both* have, what they both noticed, against the criteria/standards. (See below.)
- Confirming date, time and place for the observed lesson.
- Arranging and conducting a normal pre-lesson mentorial for the observed lesson.

DURING THE OBSERVATION

It goes without saying that you will be trying to be as unobtrusive as possible, so mentors position themselves in such a way that they are out of the way but able to see (some) pupils as well as the mentee. Mentors either ask the mentee to explain to the learners that they are there to see what's happening in the class, or when they know the particular learners, sometimes agree (in the pre-lesson mentorial) to do this themselves. They also forewarn the class that they will be scribbling a lot of notes to help them remember.

In class, mentors make as many *descriptive* notes as they can. I still divide my paper into two vertical columns and name the column on the left 'I saw ...' and the column on the right 'I heard ...' This helps me remember and acknowledge to myself and others that I am recording only descriptions, and only what 'I' noticed. (See 'On Noticing', Chapter 6).

AFTER THE LESSON

Mentors need to handle after-lesson interactions with mentees carefully. What follows are some ways mentors handle this.

- They steel themselves to resist an immediate response to any 'what did you think?' queries from the mentee in the pre-mentorial chit-chat. They may choose, perhaps, to chat about a/the learner(s) or say something like, "I can tell you what I think later if you are still interested, but I'm more interested in helping you make your own judgements. So let's go through our normal procedure and then we can consider the evidence we both have against the standards/criteria."

- They check their observation notes and make sure they are descriptive. (For example, mentors remove any judgement-revealing words such as 'too', 'very' or 'a lot of', as well as any words suggesting interpretations or judgements rather than descriptions, such as 'bored' or 'day-dreaming' or even 'low-level disruption.')
- They conduct a normal post-lesson mentorial, if time allows, using only what the mentee noticed at Step 1.
- They conduct a periodic review mentorial (see Chapter 6) and systematically go through evidence relating to each criterion/standard in turn. They start with evidence the mentee has noticed in all lessons, whether the mentor observed it or not, and, where relevant, from elsewhere in the school. Then, consulting their notes, they add anything they noticed in the lesson they observed that might confirm or contradict the emerging assessment the mentee is making. The mentor and mentee together consider the weight of evidence.

  The mentor and the mentee will both be aware that, as the mentor is charged with formal assessment, the final say is the mentor's. Nonetheless, the mentor role depends on a safe and trusting relationship (see Chapter 2), and, as my stories at the start of this chapter illustrate, observers/assessors can be wrong. So, mentors should do all they can to avoid an assessment which conflicts with their mentee's, which creates the seeming need to 'pull rank.' The mentee has been in all their lessons, whereas the mentor has only observed one. Mentors have pointed out, with obvious pleasure, those times when the mentee's assessment concurred with the one the mentor would have made based on the one observed lesson. Together, mentor and mentee agree on which standards or criteria could usefully be a focus of work in future pre- and post-lesson mentorials, particularly periodic review mentorials. These will be those standards where the joint assessment is that they need more work, and/or those where you have differing assessments.

- They review the observation experience. Ask the mentee how it felt having them in the classroom and if there is anything they can do differently next time to make him or her more comfortable and more able to focus solely on the learners and supporting their learning.
- They discuss similarities and differences between what they both noticed in the observed lesson and the likely causes (see ideas in Chapter 6).
- They fill in any paperwork together.
- They suggest the mentee engage in an 'I to why' reflection activity. Some mentors have given mentees their doubtless copious and scribbled (but edited; see above) 'observation notes' or a page or two of them. The 'I to

why' activity is one in which the mentee converts the mentor's I-statements (I saw...I heard...) into 'why' questions and considers possible answers. For example, if the mentor noted, "I heard you say 'all right, now listen to me,'" your mentee would change that to "Why did my mentor notice me saying/ Why did I say 'all right, now listen to me'?" Your mentee might then ponder possible answers, which might range from an understanding that 'getting attention' was the focus of discussion in a previous mentorial (and probably explains why their mentor noticed and noted this) to a realisation that they had alternative options which might have been more effective.

Many ToTs have noted a pattern in the results of teachers – usually student teachers – they have supported to self-assess (first). The student teachers the ToT would have rated quite highly tend to rate themselves lower, while those student teachers the ToT would have rated quite low gave themselves a higher assessment. Over time, you may find the same differences between mentees. One interpretation is that the 'better' mentee (that is, one further along on their learning journey, or better acculturated) 'knows what they don't know' and is more self-critical than they need be, whereas the 'poorer' mentee does not yet know what they don't know and may (still) be relying on 'instinctive' but outdated ways of teaching born of their past experiences as receivers of teaching. Another interpretation is that you, as assessor, and like those assessors in my own stories above, may have got things wrong. As always, what mentors do as a result of these reflections depends on the interpretation chosen which in turn depends on what else you know. I'll just note a few ideas here that mentors I know have tried.

When mentee rates low, but mentor rates higher, the mentor:

- draws the mentee's attention to all the things they *have* achieved and *can* do, in class and out; and
- reassures the mentee that there will *always,* throughout their career, be more they can learn and learn to do, and that knowing what they don't know or haven't yet mastered is already a huge step.

When the mentee rates high, but the mentor rates lower, the mentor:

- takes time to discuss the differences in assessment decisions with their mentee and generate possible interpretations and explanation of these differences, and then they let them know that they will reflect on these and get back to them;
- engages in their own SIRP to try to work out whether their mentee's assessment might be a more accurate one or not;
- works out ways to raise their mentee's awareness of those areas where the assessments differed and the mentor believes hers/his is the more

accurate – ways to help them come to know what they don't know (starting points have included, for example, lending the mentee a book and asking them to read chapter X, arranging for the mentee to observe a colleague's lesson to try to notice Y and/or resolving to suggest that the mentee might want to focus on standard Z for a few weeks); and

- lets the mentee know (some of) the outcomes of their reflections.

For 'lucky' readers

1. Supporting your mentee before an assessment

I wrote in Chapters 2 and 6 about the need to support your mentee in understanding contextual standards, not only of being a teacher, but also of their teaching. This work is helpful not only with respect to a general role of 'helping mentees into the context/system', but also as an important part of your work in helping mentees prepare to be observed and assessed while teaching. I have suggested earlier in this book that understanding these standards can be a periodic review activity (see Chapter 6). This activity will also help prepare your mentee for assessments and need not involve you in 'playing the assessor' and observing a lesson in order to do so.

Not observing classes, I have argued, will help *you* in your work with your mentee, because:

- you might more easily avoid *making* insufficiently informed judgements;
- your mentee is less likely, at the outset anyway, to *ask* for your judgements;
- you would have a valid reason for asking your mentee to describe what happened.

Table 7.1 provides yet more reasons why observing your mentee's lessons might not be a good idea (this time from the perspective of the conditions required for your mentee's learning).

2. Role-playing assessment scenarios

However, *acting* as an assessor may be helpful:

- when you have a particularly good and long-standing relationship with your mentee;
- when you judge that the mentee is now both willing and able to (and does) engage in systematic informed reflective practice alone; and
- where the mentee actually asks you to do so.

In this situation, it is nonetheless prudent to *act*, even overact, like a stern assessor (project someone very different from yourself), so that you, as supportive mentor, are as distanced from this role-played judge as possible – and you and your mentee can laugh about your acting efforts afterwards.

This type of support for your mentee may be especially useful if your system or the career stage of your mentee means that they will be subject to such assessments on a regular and/or frequent basis. Principally, this role-play will prepare them to be able to display and make (more) visible those aspects of their practice that are valued in your context and on which assessors are likely to make their judgements.

The next suggestion is also about enhancing your mentees' abilities to make contextually valued aspects of their practice (more) visible.

3. Pre-assessed-lesson preparation

The third way you can support your mentee before an assessment is through engaging in a normal, supported pre-lesson mentorial (see Chapter 6). In this 'pre-assessed-lesson' situation, the process can be extended by reference to standards and consideration of what an observer would need to notice to make favourable judgements. You might initiate this extra phase by saying something like, "Ok, that seems clear and coherent to you – and me. You have talked about what you want your pupils to learn, why and how you imagine you can help them learn it. Now, let's think from an outsider's perspective. Looking at the criteria/standards, what might an assessor notice in the lesson that you have just imagined on which they can base their judgements? Is there any way you can try to ensure they do notice this?"

Some readers might say that this just increases 'performativity' (see above), but a mentor in the Support role will want to help their mentee meet their very human need for success and achievement (see 'Basic human needs' in Chapter 8).

Mentors in the Support role may need to do all they can to ensure that the mentee is ready not only professionally but also emotionally.

4. Post-lesson fallout

Firstly and most importantly, mentors in the Support role will need to consider and attend to their mentee's affective state after the assessed lesson (see Chapters 2 and 8). Most mentors need to simply listen (actively) and reassure or congratulate. Reminding the mentee or talking about the challenges of Noticing can also be helpful (see Chapter 6). After a normal post-lesson mentorial, and where these are immediately available, the outcomes of the assessments can be considered, and decisions made on next steps.

So much for the necessary evil that is assessment by others. The next chapter returns to the life-enhancing topic of learning (which includes formative self-assessment) and considers your own learning and development as a mentor.

References

Hobson, A.J., Ashby, P., McIntyre, J. & Maldere, A. (2010), *International approaches to teacher selection and recruitment*. OECD Education Working Papers, No. 47. Paris: OECD Publishing. Accessed at: https://doi.org/10.1787/5kmbphhh6qmx-en

Hobson, A.J. & McIntyre, J. (2013), Teacher fabrication as an impediment to professional learning and development: the external mentor antidote. *Oxford Review of Education*, Vol. 39, No. 3, pp. 345–365.

Macruaic, G. & Harford, J. (2008), Researching the contested place of reflective practice in the emerging culture of performativity in schools: views from the Republic of Ireland. *European Educational Research Journal*, Vol. 7, No. 4.

8 Developing as a mentor

This chapter concerns your further 'in-service' development as a mentor, after a period of time working as the kind of mentor described in earlier chapters. There are two main sections. The first contains ideas for practices and processes you can use to support your development, alone and with others. Many of these will be familiar to you, and there may be those you thought of as you read earlier chapters of this book. Some I have already explicitly mentioned as potentially also contributing to one of your mentor roles.

The second section lists and summarises some of those conceptual tools, theories or ideas from others that may prove useful while engaging in SIRP on your own mentoring practices. They are by no means exhaustive nor always relevant, but they, as well as others included in earlier chapters (for example, 'Scaffolding' in the Introduction or 'Noticing' in Chapter 6), are ones that I and mentors I know have found pertinent and useful on more than one occasion.

1. Supporting your own development as a mentor

SIRP on mentoring

It will come as no surprise that the first practice I will list as supporting your own development as a mentor is that of your own SIRP, which I described in Chapter 6. It will support your development as a mentor as it has your development of teaching. The difference relates to how many ideas from what others say or have written you have available to use in Step 3 or Step 5. While you are likely to have plenty of resources to draw on for your teaching, which include ideas and theories you have learnt or been taught over the whole of your teaching career, you are a lot less likely to have encountered as many relevant frameworks, theories or ideas for reflecting on your mentoring practice. For this reason, I have included in the second half of this chapter, some of my own 'go-to' ideas. When I write 'my own' I do not mean that I developed these ideas, but rather that, having encountered them, I could see their relevance to my mentoring practice and that they are now in my toolkit. I use them often to help me learn from my experiences and find ways forward.

I discuss below using SIRP on your own, with the support or input of one other person and in larger groups of mentors.

DOI: 10.4324/9781003429005-9

On your own

You could, of course, engage in SIRP on your own. You'll need to set aside time for this purpose and ask yourself, for example, "So what can I learn from my experience of mentoring this week/month?" Then, think back over your experiences of mentoring since your previous reflection time and find an intriguing starting point before working through the five steps. You could use the 'mentor standards' in the appendix of this book to periodically review your work as a whole (see Chapter 6).

This will require a level of discipline and self-motivation. It is all too easy to become overwhelmed by all you have to do professionally as a teacher and a mentor as well as by demands and commitments in your private life. Teachers and mentors are givers and will often put others' needs first. I know it's a cliché, but as flight attendants remind us, we need to 'put our own oxygen mask on first before helping others.'

Working with a fellow mentor

I always find it easier to protect reflection time if I make a commitment to work with another person. Perhaps you would, too. With a buddy-mentor-colleague, you can take turns with the speaker (mentee) and listener (mentor) roles. Apart from helping ensure that you *do* engage in SIRP to develop as a mentor, working with a colleague also enhances the chances of learning from another's experiences.

One reader, who has been using SIRP for both her mentee's development and her own commented, "I have been doing this with colleagues who have completed the mentor course and do not have to be told about the steps and colleagues who haven't and then I explain the steps. I have made some great friends through co-mentoring, it creates strong bonds."

Working with your mentee

Your mentee is the closest and perhaps most immediately available collaborator in your work on your own development as a mentor, and they are the only ones who can give you feedback as receivers of your mentoring. They are also, in some respects, best placed. What's more, involving them also provides an occasion to model your professionalism (see Chapter 4) and your engagement in learning as a career-long activity. However, before I list some ideas for your mentee's involvement that mentors have used, I'd like to sound a little note of caution. Your mentee needs to concentrate on his or her own SIRP as a teacher. As the main purpose of your relationship is your mentee's development, you will need to ensure that the amount of your mentee's time you take for the purpose of your own development as a mentor does not negatively impact on time required for your mentee's development as a teacher.

What follows are a few ideas mentors I know have used which don't take up too much of your mentee's time. I have mentioned the first idea before as potentially useful in your Model role (see Chapter 4).

1. Ask for permission to record a mentorial, then later use the recording to help you re-view or visualise your mentee's reactions, while also listening carefully to the words, intonation, pauses and so on. You can then select an intriguing moment as a starting point for a SIRP process.
2. Use a recording of a mentorial to listen for and note any impacts on your mentee of your use of specific terms and bits of language (see Introduction).
3. Use a mentorial recording as a springboard for developing your listening skills:
    *   Listen to the recording and estimate Mentor Listening Time, then ask yourself if you are listening for about 80% of the time. If your talking time is more that 20%, this can be the starting point of the SIRP process, using perhaps ideas on listening given in Chapter 2 at your Step 3. If your mentee is at the beginning of their learning of SIRP, you may want to estimate your listening/talking time from Step 2, as most mentors need to ask a lot of questions to be able to see the full picture at Step 1. At this early stage working with your mentee, Step 1 can be closer to normal 50/50 conversation – say 70/30 or 60/40.
    *   Identify moments of silence in the recording. How many are there? How comfortable with these were you? How do you know? For example, you may find instances where it was you who broke the silence. Did you display trust that your mentee could and would remember or work out or come up with their own possible explanations, decisions and plans?
    *   Where your talking time was more than 20% of the total mentorial time, identify one or more of the things you said that did not seem to help your mentee (even if it helped you for one reason or another), and use this/these as starting point(s) for SIRP processes.
4. Take a minute or two to ask your mentee for help occasionally, when input from the mentee might help you decide, for example, which of the possible interpretations you generated in Step 2 reflections might be true. For example, "I was reflecting on our last mentorial, and I remembered a facial expression of yours when you were … and I said …. I thought it might mean X, Y or Z. Can you remember what you were thinking/feeling then?"

5.   Solicit the mentee's feedback (used deliberately here!) on your work. Periodically, for example, once a month on shorter programmes or once every six weeks on longer programmes, ask the mentee a limited number of questions, such as those below:

  •   What has been the most useful aspect of our work together for you?
  •   Is there anything you think I should do more or less of?
  •   Can you mention one thing you feel you have learnt?
  •   How can I help or support you better do you think?

Mentors then tell their mentee they will need a bit of time to reflect on the mentee's responses and promise to get back to them at the next mentorial.

Answers to the fourth question may result in a mentor deciding to do *exactly* as the mentee has suggested. Quite often, however, it will not. For example, when a beginning teacher mentee asks the mentor to "just tell me what to do", a mentor does take action as a result, but still doesn't tell the mentee what to do. The mentor may decide to increase activity in the Support role as a result of an interpretation of stress associated with their mentee's stage of development (see below). Such a mentor might also consider reiterating his/her reasons for not telling the mentee 'what to do' and possibly search out ways to help their mentee realise that there is no one right way of teaching. One idea for this would be to arrange for the mentee to visit a number of different colleagues' lessons. The colleagues would be ones the mentee considers to be 'good' teachers. In a discussion after the visits, it may be possible to lead the mentee to the realisation that those colleagues were not clones of each other: they were good in their own ways. The same outcome may be possible using the mentee's recollections of teachers they have had that they considered to be good.

At the end of the next mentorial, the mentor takes a bit of time to report to the mentee on the tentative decisions made as a result of the mentee's responses to the questions. How to do this will also require a little thought and preparation. You might say, for example, "So I've been reflecting on your responses to my questions last week – thanks again for that – and I've come up with some suggestions for how we might adjust our way of working together so that it suits you better. You said you find the pre-lesson mentorials most useful, so let's try having those for X% of our mentorial time for a while. I've had some other ideas too which you may notice, but time's up for today. Next time we'll have a pre-lesson mentorial so bring your plan for a lesson – one that's going to happen after our mentorial – to talk through and think more about."

Asking for information to support your *formative* assessments of your work, as above, is valuable to you as well as to the particular mentee and mentor-mentee relationship. In addition, after a period of time when mentors have worked with more than one mentee and mentees moved on, mentors have also wanted to ask for ex-mentees' *summative* feedback on their work. This can be done via an online survey which has the advantage that responses can be anonymous. This can be really useful to you as your former mentees will have had further (un-mentored) experiences and can reflect further on the medium-term impact of your work together.

Active searching

You will almost inevitably discover when considering Steps 3 and 5 that you could use more *knowledge about* mentoring, including useful practical theories as well as practices. You may decide to search online or in paper-based resources for ideas. The challenge will be, if you are following the approach set out in this book, to ensure that ideas you come across are consistent with the ONSIDE, non-judgemental reflective approach you are engaged in (see Introduction). There are many, many meanings attached to the word 'mentoring' out there, and these meanings are not always made explicit. Few, if any, that I am aware of actually support the learning of teaching-learnacy, and many, given the practices they espouse, might best, in my view, be described by a different label (for example, supervisor, assessor or trainer) even if the interactions *are* carried out on a one-to-one basis.

While you are most likely to engage in this active searching alone, the 'sharing practical theories' activity proposed in the next section can save all of you a lot of time. You will hear ideas that colleagues have not only found, but also found practically useful.

Wider sharing

When you, your scheme leader or your original mentor trainer can organise a reflection meeting for the whole cohort of mentors in your scheme or institution, there are further opportunities for learning.

As with all 'whole group' meetings, the value is as much in the opportunities for networking and enhancing group cohesion as in the formal programme of activities chosen, whether from those described below or those you may create. It will therefore be important to allow enough time for chat, over coffee or lunch perhaps. Your time together also needs to feel leisurely, a safe space without pressure, and include moments of 'fun', perhaps in your random grouping and regrouping processes between activities (see 'Modes of mind' below). You will probably have your own ideas for fun grouping activities, but if these are not in your toolkit of teaching practices, you can find many described in Malderez and Bodóczky, 1999.

Most pair-work or group-work activities in such gatherings will use SIRP as a basis. Some will benefit from some level of participants' preparatory work. The main activities on a plan for a day-long meeting I was involved in were as follows. This was with a group that had been working together since their initial mentor training and who had mentioned in the pre-meeting preparation that they were 'most looking forward to getting the group's perspective on recent challenges.'

- Sticky moments
- Light-bulb moments
- Sharing practical theories – useful and used
- What next?

Detailed descriptions of each of the activities listed above follow, which you could choose from or adapt to include in your meetings.

Sticky moments

Aims: To help all participants realise that such moments face us all; they are not alone.

To enable new perspectives to shed light on the issues discussed.

Timing: At about a quarter to a half of the way through the whole mentoring process or after at least four weeks of mentoring.

Time needed: 1 hour and 30 minutes to 2 hours

Materials

1. written description of a 'sticky moment' per participant.

Participants were asked to recall a moment in their mentoring when they felt (maybe only initially) taken aback or stuck for how to respond to something they noticed or that happened in the mentoring process. They were then asked to write and submit beforehand a Step 1 description of that moment, keeping the identity of the participants confidential.

Procedure

1. In friendship groups of three, participants pass their written sticky moments round the group, until all have read all three stories.
2. The group decides who is 'A', who is 'B' and who is 'C' and starts with focus on the story from 'A.'
3. 'A' listens as the other two ('B' and 'C') talk through the four remaining steps as if they were the mentor engaging in SIRP.
4. 'A' shares with 'B' and 'C' the conclusions she/he actually arrived at (Steps 4 and 5) and what happened subsequently.

5. Any differences between interpretations and decisions reached by 'A' and 'B&C' are discussed.
6. Steps 3 to 5 above are repeated twice more, with stories from 'B' and then 'C' in focus.
7. The group agrees to some items on a 'What we've learnt from this exercise' list to report to the whole group.
8. Each small group spokesperson reports to the whole group on what their group has learnt.

Alternatives

*   Preparation

    One alternative might be to ask participants to recall a sticky moment in-session. The advantage of this alternative, of not asking mentors to *write* about the event, is, of course, that you can avoid overburdening already very busy colleagues. However, there are drawbacks, too. Firstly, for the participants, the pressure of time in session seems to make it difficult for some to recall sticky moments. Secondly, without the written record, it makes it harder for those who start with another's Step 1 description to imagine themselves into the situation enough to easily work through the steps. Finally, without hard copies of the sticky moments, the convenor cannot as easily recognise common issues to make the focus of future meetings.

    Such descriptions might usefully also be passed to the first mentor trainer who was responsible for participants' preparation as mentors (where this is not the same person as the convenor of the wider sharing meeting). The fact that the mentors encountered specific types of 'sticky moments' can act as feedback to the mentor trainer who may on reflection then decide to make adjustments to future mentor preparation programmes.

*   Procedure

    When time allows, or when there are 'fast finisher' groups, and where different decisions are made by the two group members and the original mentor:

    Participants 'act out' the different/new decision (made by one or both of the two 'B' and 'C' group members who were not the original mentor), in a role-play. The original mentor, whose sticky moment story is the focus, takes the mentee role, and one of the others acts as the mentor carrying out the step five decisions made in the earlier discussion.

    In some programmes where the mentors have a more limited time to meet as a whole group, this type of role-play has been such a useful activity, that almost all the time was devoted to this extended 'sticky moments' activity. This type of role-play can enable the mentors to enhance their understanding of their mentees through having to put themselves in their mentees' shoes, help them realise the possible impacts of different decisions and enable them all to witness different mentoring styles.

Light-bulb moments

Aims: To enable participants to share the new understandings that experience has given them.

Timing: After at least four weeks of mentoring

Time needed: 30 to 45 minutes

Materials (preparation)

All participants will need pen and paper to make a few preparatory notes.

Procedure

1. In random groups of three to five participants, first make notes silently and individually on any 'light-bulb' moments – times when something hit home, or they came to a realisation or a new understanding. Participants should note *what* hit home or what they realised and what the circumstances were or *when* it happened.
2. Participants take turns telling each other what they realised and when.
3. The group discusses commonalities and differences in their realisations – their 'whats' – before going on to discuss how they had come to their realisations.
4. The group agrees on what they will report to the whole group from the activity.
5. Spokespeople from each group take turns reporting to the whole group.

Sharing practical theories – useful and used

Aims: To enable participants to share the new practical theories they have discovered which are now in their personal toolkits.

Timing: After at least eight weeks of mentoring

Time needed: 45 minutes to 1 hour and 30 minutes (depending on size of the whole group)

Materials (preparation)

All participants will need pen and paper to make a few preparatory notes.

Procedure

1. In random groups of three to five participants, first make notes silently and individually on ideas recalled or found for Step 3 of their SIRP experiences which they found useful.
2. Group members take turns telling each other the ideas and the circumstances in which they were useful.
3. The group then agrees on one or two ideas that they think would be most useful to share with the whole group.

4. Groups take turns sharing the idea(s) with the whole group. A spokesperson, or the member(s) who came across the chosen idea(s), reports.

What next?

This activity is not about individual mentor development but rather about the development of the particular mentor programme.

Aims: To enable participants to contribute to the ongoing shaping and development of the programme they are engaged in.

Timing: Half way through and at the end of time spent mentoring the same mentee.

Time needed: 45 minutes to 1 hour and 30 minutes (depending on size of the whole group)

Materials (preparation)

All participants will need pen and paper to make a few preparatory notes.

Procedure

1. In random groups, participants list things that supported their mentoring and things that hindered their mentoring.
2. Group members take turns sharing their lists.
3. Group members discuss and agree on any adaptations or changes they would like to see in their programme as a whole. They may consider, for example, mentee/mentor selection, pairings, length of time for mentoring and conditions such as time allowances for the work, timetabling, venues for mentorials and other physical conditions, as well as wider support for mentoring, mentor development and possibly mentor accreditation.
4. Group members then agree to one or two 'proposals for change.'
5. Groups take turns making their proposals, which are listed and voted on by the group as a whole.
6. Small groups are then asked to consider the top proposals (the ones receiving the greater numbers of votes) and agree to any 'next steps' needed to achieve the agreed-upon tweaks or changes to their programme to benefit mentees, mentors and the immediate or broader context.
7. Groups take turns sharing their 'next steps' ideas with the whole group.
8. The whole group then decides *who* will take the agreed-upon next steps, by *when* and *how* the outcomes will be shared.

This activity has resulted in, for example:

*   a whole staff meeting with mentoring as the topic and a mentor and a mentee talking about their work together and what they individually gained

from it (where mentors complained of a lack of understanding by colleagues of what they were doing);

- a request to the headteacher about timetabling (where mentors found they had to schedule mentorial time after work as their timetables clashed);
- the inclusion of a session about mentoring, with mentors present and mingling, in an induction period for new members of staff (so that future mentees might have a slightly more informed choice of mentor); and
- the attendance of the mentor at meetings of the parents of pupils taught by their mentee (to allay any fears and explain that even though they were not actually observing classes, they were following closely and very aware of what was happening, and that the way they were working was much more likely to lead to better and more confident teaching sooner).

If the leader of the meeting was not the mentor coordinator, it is also useful to forward the whole list of proposals to her or him.

Finally, the choice and sequencing of activities for 'wider sharing' meetings does, of course, and as always, depend on context. For example, if attendees are not yet a group, in the psychosocial sense, starting with 'sticky moments' may feel threatening. I wonder if this, in part, lay behind the comments of one of my draft readers. She didn't comment on the 'Sticky moments' section but wrote about 'Light-bulb moments':

> I would expect that mentors would be more excited about sharing these, they would be more likely perhaps to think of these moments beforehand, since they bring back good memories. It's an opportunity to share their knowledge, and perhaps what might have motivated someone to start mentoring in the first place.

In some contexts, participants in the meeting also include mentees, and the time available is more limited. In such cases, perhaps the most appropriate activity above would be 'Light-bulb moments.' So, if you are organising and planning for a wider sharing meeting, apart from considerations about how long it can be, where you can hold it and so on, do consider carefully who the participants are and how what you propose to do can support their achievement of basic psychological needs (see below).

2. Practical theories

The following theories are a 'starter set' of practical theories which have proved useful to recall in Step 3 for mentors I know. As well as giving a brief description of the framework, I also describe the kinds of contexts in which they have proved helpful to mentors as they work to decide on an interpretation of an event and/or work out their next move. Most of the ideas I include here relate to the work of understanding your mentee so that the context of your relationship is as conducive to your mentee's learning as you can make it and your actions relevant and supportive to the particular needs of your mentee.

These theories are:

- Scaffolding
- Noticing
- Reflective practice
- Stages of teacher development
- Claxton's three 'modes of mind'
- Basic psychological needs
- Relationships and goals
- Flow

The first three topics in this list have been summarised elsewhere in the book, so here I simply note where, and give one or more references for further reading. For the remainder of topics listed, I summarise the main useful ideas before giving some examples of how mentors have used them in their own SIRP on mentoring. As these summaries are, of course, just one reader's interpretations (my own) of complex ideas, you may benefit from going back to the original sources when you have time.

Scaffolding

See Introduction or, for a fuller explanation, see Malderez and Wedell, 2007.

Noticing

See Chapter 6, Mason, 2001.

Reflective practice

See Chapter 6, Introduction, Schon, 1987.

Stages of teacher development

Two main ideas have proved useful to mentors. One relates mainly to beginning-teacher mentees, and the other largely to mentees who are further along in their teaching careers.

Beginning-teacher mentees

A number of researchers (e.g., Kagan, 1992) have attempted to characterise stages in beginning-teacher development.

A simple useful summary of cumulative stages is as follows:

Stage One: focus on self-as-a-teacher

Stage Two: focus on self-as-a-teacher *and* learners' behaviour

Stage Three: focus on self-as-a-teacher, learners' behaviour *and* learners' learning

Step 1 in a mentee's SIRP is particularly useful for diagnosing your beginning-teacher mentee's stage of development. What follows are some very rough and oversimplified generalisations.

Mentees who describe 'what happened' in terms of only or mainly what they, as teachers, did and said, who often simply talk through a kind of oral lesson plan where the main pronoun used is 'I', are likely to be at the start of this development process, at Stage One.

Mentees who also mention pupil misbehaviour (behaviour that is the easiest to notice because it is unexpected and unwanted – see 'Noticing in Chapter 6) are a little further along. When mentees also mention signs of 'good' behaviour, they have progressed further to Stage Two.

Mentees are at Stage Three if they also mention what pupils say or do or display in facial expressions, for example, that can be related to engagement, understanding or lack of it or learning and achievement.

The mentor's questions at Step 1, asked so that the mentor can get a clear picture of what happened, can eventually help the mentee move on. This relies on the mentor genuinely listening, visualising and then asking those questions they need to have answers to in order to complete their own mental picture or video of the particular moment in the lesson that the mentee has chosen as their focus. If my mentee seems to be at Stage One and only tells me what she/he did and said, I *need* to ask about what the pupils said or did in order for me to 'see' what happened. At the same time, I signal to my mentee that I value re-viewing and reflecting on what the learners – all of them, not just the 'problematic' ones – said or did. Over time, having been made aware that there is more to notice, and making the effort to notice the things I ask about, my mentee volunteers this information. Similarly, I might ask whether my mentee noticed anything in pupil behaviour that might indicate whether or not learning was occurring or had happened. The question in Step 5 about what a mentee might need to notice to be able to assess whether a chosen strategy had 'worked' or not and the need to consciously think about this may also help a mentee begin to notice the all-important learning-related feedback pupils give all the time.

More-experienced teacher mentees

It is also worthwhile thinking about the 'stages of development' described above with more-experienced teachers, too, I have found.

Changes of context, for example, can mean that such teachers may revert to being closer to Stage One, as they seek to fit in and be accepted. In such cases, mentors might want to increase their focus on their Acculturator role.

There were also some people who, even though they had worked as a teacher for several or even many years, seemed to me to be stuck on Stage Two. This, I think, is unsurprising if they are products of contexts which treated teachers as technicists (rather than professionals), requiring them to enact others' decisions and plans and leading them to expect and wait for others to make judgements on their work. They came from contexts which had not supported teachers' development of learnacy, in many cases despite claims to the contrary, and in which even their continued employment depended on assessments of visible behaviours against limited 'universal best practice' criteria. No wonder Huberman (1993) found many mid-career teachers in states of cynicism or complacency. The key to emerging from these states, according to Huberman, is constant gentle 'tinkering' with what they do and how they do things in classrooms – in other words, professional learning.

While writing the paragraph above, I was reminded of the example of two teachers who had worked ten years as teachers. It was said that one had ten years' experience and was an experienced teacher, while the other had one years' experience ten times. The difference is that the first had learned from their experience. I recalled this idea as being one 'in the ether' for decades, but I may well have adopted it from Penny Ur (1996, p. 317).

With these 'stuck', cynical or complacent teachers, SIRP taught them how to take charge of their own development, process experience and begin to tinker with things in their classes. The mentoring process gave them learnacy, agency, professionalism and a renewed enthusiasm for teaching.

Incidentally, research has shown (Hobson et al., 2009; Malderez and Bodóczky, 1997) that your choice to become a mentor is likely to result in your own renewed enthusiasm for the teaching profession, too, as you engage with the learning processes and interactions with mentee-colleagues that mentoring entails.

Claxton's three 'modes of mind'

I have created the table below from some key ideas in G. Claxton (1997). His ideas were among those I found very relevant when thinking about how to support teacher learning, which led eventually to, for example, the five-step SIRP protocol (see Malderez and Wedell, 2007). Claxton argues that there are three main ways we use our minds. Professionals, including teachers, ideally use all three. I'll try to explain them a bit more, but let's start with the table.

Table 8.1 Modes of mind

Modes of mind	Characteristics	
1. Fast Mind We say people who are good at using this kind of mind *can think on their feet*.	Works when in the midst of activity. Doesn't use language/logic, etc. - no time. Uses intuition, 'gut' feelings/hunches (products of 'slow mind' work).	Used when teaching. Direct link with undermind - explains why we teach as we were taught, rather than as we were taught/told to teach.
2. D-Mode The 'd' stands for **deliberative** and also for **default** - because this mode of mind is the 'default' meaning of 'think' when we say, for example, "let me think about that." It is also the meaning of 'think' in the subtitle of Claxton's book. We say people who are good at using this kind of mind are *clever*.	Works when we consciously employ it to 'work things out' or 'think.' Uses logic and language. Doesn't need as much time as the slow mind, but more than the fast mind.	Uses conscious personal theories, as well as public theories or ideas of others. Is the mode of mind used in mentorials.
3. Slow Mind ('undermind') We say people who are good at using this kind of mind are *wise*.	Works on experiences (of activity/practice) 'without our knowing.' Allows 'learning by osmosis', from experience, which bypasses words. Needs time to be 'fed' and to work. Needs leisure, fun, fantasy or metaphor to surface to consciousness.	Creates values, attitudes and beliefs, which are often unconscious and 'taken-for granted.' We can become conscious of products of undermind work in certain circumstances - with leisure or those activities involving fun, fantasy or metaphor.

Claxton explains how we all use our minds in three main ways according to, at least in part and predictably, context of use. Developing as a professional teacher requires the use of all three modes of mind.

Fast Mind

When we have 'no time' to 'think', as in d-mode (see Table 8.1 above), we use our Fast Mind. Examples of when we routinely use our Fast Mind are when we cross a road or when, in the midst of teaching, we 'automatically' respond or react to some learner behaviour. In both examples, there is no time to stop and work out what to do. There is no time to calculate speeds of traffic and the speed you would need to walk to get safely across the road, you just have to look and go. There is not enough time in a busy classroom either. We can't freeze the action and recall various theories on, for example, error correction and the pros and cons of various types of response to learner errors. We just need to react in one way or another (including deliberately displaying no visible reaction). In both examples, how we react also depends on what we notice. Experiences in which we use our Fast Minds 'feed' Slow Mind, or Undermind, work. There is a direct link between these two modes of mind. To me, this direct but wordless link explains the responses to my requests for teachers to explain why they had done something in class, which were so often along the lines of "I don't know really, it just *felt* right."

Slow Mind

As with Fast Mind, we are not usually very conscious that our Undermind or Slow Mind is or has been working, as both the Fast Mind and the Undermind work 'wordlessly' and 'without our knowing.' In contrast to the Fast Mind which has split seconds to work, the Undermind needs a lot of time. There are certain circumstances in which insights on our experiences (including our D-Mode work) from Undermind work can surface into our consciousness. These involve leisure, fun, fantasy and metaphor. Most of us, I am sure, have had the experience of that name we'd forgotten suddenly popping into our heads over breakfast the following morning, or of ways forward on particular issues occurring to us while taking a walk or gardening. The leisure of the night's sleep, our walk or favourite pastime had allowed our Undermind to not only continue its work, but also to let us know the outcomes. Our mothers were wise when they advised us to 'sleep on it'!

D-Mode

Claxton says that this mode of mind, which is conscious, uses words and logic and needs some time (more than Fast Mind, but less than the Slow Mind). Using our D-Mode mind is what we usually mean by 'think.' It is the mode of mind we use when reading 'theories' or working out when, how or whether we might use them. It is the mode of mind you are using now reading this. It is the main obvious mode of mind I used writing this book.

The subtitle to Claxton's book – "why intelligence increases when we think less" – uses this meaning of 'think' and suggests we need to pay attention to providing conditions for all three modes of mind to be able to work – and to work in harmony. However, it is all too easy for any practitioners to rely mostly or more on the automatic Undermind–Fast Mind–Undermind process only (as do the teachers with ten years in post who teach one year ten times). This can make it very difficult for new ideas generated by others (accessed through D-Mode thinking) to have any impact, or for teachers to be truly professionals and keep up to date (see Chapter 4). In part, this also explains why this book has taken so long to write. I needed to allow plenty of time for my Undermind to work on all my past experiences and for walks and gardening and for many good long sleeps so that outcomes of this Undermind work could emerge into my consciousness! I have lost count of the number of times I have woken up with ideas and insights I wanted to include in this book.

Use in mentoring

The protocols described in Chapter 6 take into account these ideas and potentially call on heart (Undermind), hand (Fast Mind) as well as 'head' (D-Mode). To a certain extent, this depends rather on how a mentor guides the use of these protocols and/or reflects on their use.

In Step 2, one reason for brainstorming as many interpretations as possible, including fanciful, crazy or playful ones, is that this can challenge the 'taken for granted' ideas and may allow products of Undermind work to emerge.

As noted above, there is a natural 'wordless' link between experience or practice and the work of the Undermind on previous experiences. However, the linking of others' theories (public theories) to the often wordless personal theories generated by the Undermind is much more difficult. Steps 3 and 4 require the folding into or linking into a teacher's broader thinking of such public theories and supports them in fulfilling the requirement of a professional to 'keep up to date' in practice, not just in rhetoric, in what they *do* and not simply the words they use.

Step 5 and pre-lesson mentorials encourage imagining, fantasising/thinking forward which can allow products of Undermind work to emerge and may further challenge the 'taken for granted' ideas.

So, *all* teachers' practices are underpinned by their personal theories, whether or not they can articulate them. For them, there is no gap, just coherence. The 'problem' of the 'theory-practice' gap is a 'problem' only for others (researchers, teachers of teachers) as well as for the profession. Reflective practice has, since Schön's seminal work in the 1980s, long been seen as a way to close that gap and professionalise teachers. To do so, though, it needs to be more than simply 'thinking about' a lesson or a course afterwards, or even filling in a box on 'reflections', and it needs to be taught (Bardhun, 1998). This for me is a/the major and vital role for mentors in post-lesson mentorials.

Use in SIRP on mentoring

Mentors have, reflecting on a period of serious and earnest endeavour and on recalling the modes of mind, decided they needed to be more patient and lighthearted with themselves as well as with their mentee.

One decided to shelve thinking about a particular sticky moment and take herself off for a walk.

Another, as well as being more patient with her mentee, resolved to inject more fun into the relationship and work. I will describe next one quick activity for doing this, which almost always generates laughter as well as sometimes creative new ideas (described in Malderez and Bodóczky, 1999) and which can often fit into the end of a mentorial. However, fun can be had also in simple interactions and is often more a question of attitude and personality, your own as well as your mentee's. So, if you know yourself to be, or appear to be, very serious or stern, you may have to make a conscious effort to 'lighten up' sometimes. Fun is a serious business! (Also see the next section, 'Basic psychological needs.')

Change the words and imagine

Firstly, take one statement from your mentee's Step 1 description and 'play' by replacing one key word with another (and making subsequent necessary linguistic changes) then imagining possible impacts and outcomes. Once your mentee has understood the process, they can take over changing words.

For example:

Original: I walked into the room and said 'good morning.'

I 'walked' can become: I ran/danced/hopped/crawled...

I walked 'into the room' can become: I walked to the back of the room/ around the room...

I walked into the room and 'said' can become: I walked into the room and mouthed/shouted/whispered/screamed/sang...

'And said "good morning"' can become:... and a student wrote 'good morning' on the board.

This activity is then followed by a quick consideration of which of the ideas generated could be practically useful to the mentee. For example, a mentor might say "That was fun! But there may be some serious ideas there you could consider. Did you spot any?" The mentee could reply, for example, "Well, I was thinking about the value of surprising my learners sometimes," or "I can see it would be useful to move around the room more often."

After a quick 'change the words' activity and discussion, one mentee decided to move out from behind the teacher's desk more often, another to vary how they started a class and another to ask students to write on the board more often.

Basic psychological needs

The psychiatrist William Glasser (Choice Theory, 1998) claims that striving to meet five basic psychological needs, discussed below, motivates *all* human behaviour. When we are unable to meet these needs, all our behaviour is focused on trying to do so. When these needs are met, we can concentrate on other things – such as learning.

1. Security and survival

In most mentoring situations, mentees can meet their needs for physical security and survival. The focus here will be more on enabling our mentees to feel safe psychologically. In mentoring, this is done, for example, through ensuring confidentiality, being non-judgemental and making sure the programme is seen as being for *any* teacher and not for poorly performing ones. Having said that, hungry or thirsty mentees will probably not get the most out of mentorials.

I recall conducting a mentorial in the bush in Botswana where large wild animals roamed, creating a situation that was physically rather insecure – for me at least. However, it was psychologically safe as I was not a line manager and we were away from others' ears.

2. Belonging and love

We meet our needs for belonging and love with our family and friends. We can also meet the need for belonging in our workplaces with colleagues. Time, familiarity and many interactions are required for this sense of belonging to occur at work. The Acculturator and Supporter roles of a mentor can support mentees in developing this sense of belonging.

3. Freedom and choices

The type of mentoring described in this book ensures that all mentees can meet their needs for freedom and choices, as at no point does the mentor tell the mentee what to do. In addition, participation for many mentees is voluntary, and it may also be possible for mentees to choose the mentor they work with, although in many contexts this choice will not be possible.

4. Success and power

We all have a need to feel we have achieved something. Arguably a teacher's main role and therefore goal is to enable all his or her students to learn all of the time. Yet I don't know a single one of us who can claim to have fully fulfilled this role or reached this goal. In that sense, we can be seen as being unsuccessful. Yet we can and do achieve many smaller successes as we strive to attain this larger goal.

The type of mentoring described in this book is empowering by definition. Successes – in making appropriate decisions which 'work', in tinkering, in learning to use and find the value in SIRP, in making progress towards larger, if interim, goals – can be celebrated by both mentor and mentee.

5. Fun

All humans need some fun and opportunities to meet our needs for fun. We know this applies to children as they learn through play. As we get older and are reprimanded for making 'inappropriate' choices for behaviours aimed at meeting our needs for fun in classrooms, we often lose access to this powerful route to learning. If teachers can offer more appropriate in-classroom opportunities for students to meet their needs for fun, 'misbehaviour' can be reduced. Many learners are still also 'learning adulthood', after all, so of course they will make mistakes in this as well as in everything else they are learning.

By the time we become adults, we have been conditioned to think that 'fun' is something that happens, and should happen, mostly outside of work or learning situations. However, most teachers are very busy with the serious business of work and family demands, and they may feel they have few opportunities to meet their needs for fun. Yet, we have seen the serious value of 'fun' (see 'Modes of mind' above) in teacher and mentor development. Mentors need to provide as many opportunities as possible for mentees to also meet their needs for fun.

We all have many ways in which we can meet our basic needs. The need to be able to make appropriate choices about how to meet those needs whatever the circumstances explains Glasser's term 'Choice Theory' for his work.

Use in SIRP on mentoring

As seeking to explain and interpret behaviour is the main task in Step 2, I hope it is easy to see why this practical theory is so useful in SIRP on mentoring as well as on teaching.

Here are two examples of ways in which mentors have found it useful to recall basic psychological needs.

One mentor reflecting on some mentee behaviour wondered whether it might be due to tensions between attempting to meet needs for success while also meeting her needs for belonging, both of which require time. The mentor resolved to pay more attention to the Acculturator role so that their mentee might meet some needs for belonging at work. She also resolved to pay more attention to helping the mentee notice and celebrate the little achievements and progress towards the mentee's main goals. This might enable the mentee to meet needs for success and allow them to reclaim some time to devote to the family and meet needs for belonging.

Another mentor realised that unusual mentee behaviour was probably due to where the mentorial had taken place – within earshot of others – which had made it impossible for the mentee to meet security needs.

Relationships and goals

These ideas are ones Caroline (Bodòczky) and I discovered when we were creating our first mentor development courses 30 years ago. They are ones I and mentors I have worked with have returned to again and again.

D.W. Johnson (1981) describes different behaviours which can be appropriate in life in general, depending on the importance of both the relationship and the goal. He equates each different type of behaviour with an animal and a verb.

In the explanations below, I give examples. However, in mentoring, where *both* the relationship and the goal(s) are always of high importance, there is only one way to be. I hope readers of this book will easily be able see how mentor behaviour in any of the first four ways would be inappropriate in almost all mentoring situations.

1. For Teddy Bears, the relationship is very important, but achieving their own goal has no real importance to them, so they *give in*.
    Example: I'm a mother. It's a Saturday. I want to read my book (my goal). My children want me to take them to the park. We go to the park.
2. A Tortoise *withdraws* from both the relationship and efforts to achieve their goal. Neither the relationship nor their goal is important to them.
    Example: I decide to walk home through the park. A stranger comes up and pesters me. I go out to the road and take a bus home.

3. A Shark *forces* things to achieve their goal and sacrifices the relationship which has little importance to the shark.

    Example: I'm a used car salesman. I push to get the best price.

4. A Fox *compromises* as both the goal and the relationship have some importance, but not a high importance in either case.

    Example: As a politician I must keep voters and keep a reasonable relationship with them, so I will amend goals as necessary. I am also prepared to lose some voters in order to achieve some or some parts of my goals.

5. An Owl is wise (in Western cultures at least!). An Owl knows that both relationships and goals are very important, so they *communicate* about their own goal and the goal of the other until together they can arrive at a way to make it possible for both to achieve their goals.

    Example: A teenager is rebelling against the curfew set by his or her parents. The relationship with their child is as important as achieving their goals, so the parents initiate a discussion. They ask for and listen to their child's goals (perhaps to be able to stay to the end of a particular activity, or to be like their friends) and explain their own (for example, to ensure that their child has enough sleep on a school night and/or that the child is at home before dark, for safety reasons.) They know (and perhaps explain) that they do also want their child to learn adulthood, and for this the child needs opportunities to learn to be responsible for their own decisions and the consequences of them. For this reason, the parents ask the child how she/he thinks they can all achieve their goals. Resolutions might include, for example, that the curfew is extended on non-school nights and/or that the parents will pick them up on such occasions to bring them home.

    Mentoring example: teachers and mentors must be 'owly' too. They must achieve the goal of promoting learning. It's their job. In order to do their job, they must also create and keep a good relationship with learners. So, a mentor, when their relationship with a mentee seems strained, reflects carefully (perhaps using ideas in this list) and talks with the mentee about needs and goals (again), their own and those of their mentee. This often results in strengthened relationships and a 'win–win' situation where both can achieve their goals.

Use in SIRP on mentoring

Mentors noticing a less-conducive atmosphere in their relationship with their mentees (often around the midpoint in their mentoring), and recalling these ideas, have decided to revisit the goals agreed to in their first meeting. They ensure they are open about their own goals and any difficulties they are experiencing in making progress towards them and invite the mentee to do the same. Many mentors discover their mentees' goals have shifted over time. This may be because the mentee knows more about what they don't know at this point in the mentoring process, or because the mentees did not yet feel safe enough to reveal their actual goals at the outset. Some mentors have also included meeting one or more 'basic needs' (see above) as goals in this conversation. The aim is to conclude with a revised set of goals and an agreed-upon set of ways forward, which both can see are achievable.

Some new mentors have realised that they have been behaving in rather sharklike ways, while others, perhaps in prioritising their Support role over their Educator role, have been rather too much like teddy bears.

Flow

Csikszentmihalyi's sociological research (1997) broadly set out to discover what makes people content in their lives. He found that the more moments of what he termed 'flow' a person experienced, the more content the life. 'Flow' occurs when we are engaged in activities containing challenges that we have just about enough skills to accomplish with persistence. To me, this pushing of our boundaries is clearly about learning, about taking a next step on a learning journey. The task stretches us and requires effort but is not so difficult that we can't do it and meet our needs for success.

Csikszentmihalyi also found that periods of flow are characterised by us being so engaged in what we are doing that we 'don't notice time passing.' We hope all those whose learning we support, whether as teachers or mentors, are 'engaged.' These ideas can help us think about whether the tasks we set had or have enough or too much challenge given the skill sets of our students, as a group and as individuals.

Csikszentmihalyi describes other emotional states which vary according to the relationships between challenge and skills. For example, people with low levels of skill can feel and display, in low to high levels of challenge, apathy, worry or anxiety. Those with some skills, but not high levels of skill, might feel and display, in low to high levels of challenge, boredom or 'arousal'/excitement. People with high levels of skill, experience and display, in the context of low to high levels of challenge, relaxation, control or finally flow. It is worth noting that another defining characteristic of flow is that it is not associated with a particular emotion at the time it is occurring, although a person will be energised and satisfied after the event.

(Incidentally, in my story about 'The Day the Tutor Came' at the beginning of the previous chapter, it seems clear to me now, looking through the lens of Csikszentmihalyi's ideas, that at the start of the lesson I was in a state of 'arousal'/excitement.)

Use in mentoring

These ideas can be particularly useful when the mentee is considering others' potentially useful ideas at Step 3 which may shed light on Step 2 interpretations that include any of the emotions given above.

Use in SIRP on mentoring

Mentors recalling these ideas have decided, for example, when interpreting some mentee behaviour as exhibiting anxiety (suggesting that the challenges their mentee is facing are currently higher than the mentee's skills), to increase their own interventions in their Support role, to give more time to pre-lesson mentorials and to ensure as far as possible that any assessments are postponed. Where the mentor and mentee identify a lack in particular skills, the mentor may also add, temporarily, a 'trainer' role. Especially in the early career years, the demands of teaching can feel overwhelming, and the mentee, faced with so many things they need to learn about and how to do, can fail to notice what they do know and do know how to do. Therefore, for the sake of the mentee's well-being, apart from reassuring talk in their Support role, for example, mentors may also determine to ensure that post-lesson mentorials focus more frequently on something that the mentee seemed pleased about.

At the other end of the scale, mentors noticing signs of relaxation in their mentee have nudged their mentee to continue learning by taking on new challenges or greater responsibilities – from trying out a new strategy in class to being a presenter or co-presenter at a meeting or conference.

In Chapter 9, I look at the idea of 'stories' as way of understanding teacher knowledge, but mainly in order to offer you some examples of metaphorical stories which mentors have found useful to experience as part of their development (see Introduction). Reading and working with these can allow you to change your 'mode of mind' (see above) and, I hope, offer you some relaxation and even fun after all this hard D-Mode work you have been doing!

References

Bardhun, S. (1998), *Traits and conditions that accelerate teacher learning*. Unpublished doctoral dissertation. London: Thames Valley University.

Claxton, G. (1997), *Hare brain tortoise mind: why intelligence increases when you think less*. London: Fourth Estate.

Csikszentmihalyi, M. (1997), *Finding flow: the psychology of engagement with everyday life*. New York: Basic Books.

Glasser, W. (1998), *Choice theory: a new psychology of personal freedom*. New York: Harper Collins.

Hobson, A.J., Ashby, P., Malderez, A.& Tomlinson, P.D. (January 2009), Mentoring beginning teachers: what we know and what we don't. *Teaching and Teacher Education*, Vol. 25, No. 1, pp. 207-216.

Huberman, M. (1993), *The lives of teachers*. London: Cassell.

Johnson, D.W. (1981), *Reaching out: interpersonal effectiveness and self-actualisation*. Englewood Cliffs, NJ: Prentice-Hall.

Kagan, D.M. (1992), Professional growth among preservice and beginning teachers. *Review of Educational Research*, Vol. 62, No. 2, pp. 129-169.

Malderez, A.& Bodoczky, C. (1997), The INSET impact of a mentoring course. In D. Hayes (Ed.) *In-service teacher development: international perspectives*. London: Prentice Hall.

Malderez, A.& Bodóczky, C. (1999), *Mentor courses: a resource book for trainer trainers*. Cambridge: Cambridge University Press.

Malderez, A. & Wedell, M. (2007), *Teaching teachers: processes and practices*. London: Continuum.

Mason, J. (2001), *Researching your own practice: the discipline of noticing*. London: Routledge.

Schon, D. (1987), *Educating the reflective practitioner*. San Francisco, CA: Jossey-Bass.

Ur, P. (1996), *A course in language teaching: practice and theory*. Cambridge: Cambridge University Press.

9 Stories

This chapter is also intended for further mentor development, after a period of mentoring in the manner described in the earlier chapters. Here, I look at the concept of 'stories' in two ways. The first is as way of understanding teacher knowledge. The second is simply as the oldest didactic tool we have, which I believe is as useful and powerful now as it ever was. My main purpose is to offer you a few of the allegorical stories which mentors have found useful to experience and which have contributed to their development (see Introduction). I hope reading and working with these can allow you to change your 'mode of mind' (see Chapter 8) and offer you some relaxation or even fun. This may be sorely needed after all the hard D-Mode work you have been doing while reading the rest of the book!

I present three stories. After reading a story, I ask you to ponder the messages you can take from the story for your work as a mentor. A brief section discussing differences between listening to storytelling events and reading stories follows, with descriptions of how I and others prepare to *tell stories* such as these. Finally, I provide brief commentaries on each story. The commentaries include the messages other mentors have taken from each story and are placed deliberately (to give physical space for your own messages to occur to you and in quiz-book fashion) at the end of the chapter. Having said that, you may want to stop reading when you have read one or more stories and resume your reading the next day, after a good sleep, to allow more insights to occur to you.

Stories and teacher knowledge

Elbaz, in an early paper discussing the storied nature of teacher knowledge, defines 'story' as "the very stuff of teaching, the landscape within which we live as teachers...and within which the work of teachers can be seen as making sense" (Elbaz, 1991, p. 3). To me, SIRP-ing allows the creation of tellable (is that a word?!) stories of teaching, which are, in this sense, representations of new knowledge. What's more, as they are now consciously known to me, I can now *tell* my stories and they become available for reshaping, that is, for further learning. SIRP can also help mentees to surface their hidden, unknown and therefore previously untellable stories. Stories are, in their content, contextualised in all senses of the word (see Chapter 1). In addition, the form – *how* we tell, or write our stories – is contextualised too, whether or not any further learning

DOI: 10.4324/9781003429005-10

has occurred and the content been adjusted. The stories I tell today are not the same as the ones I told a year ago or to a different audience.

Stories in mentoring and mentor development

I wrote in the introduction to this chapter that stories are perhaps the oldest didactic tool we have, and there are two kinds of stories that are useful to tell in this context. The first are stories from the real-life experiences of teachers and mentors, to use as examples, or in the Model role. (I have used many of my own stories of this kind in this book.) The second are the allegorical stories, such as those below, which can provide opportunities for the products of Undermind work to surface into consciousness and reshape our stories. When told rather than read or read aloud (see below), they can also, for example, provide variety and a welcome break from group-work when groups of mentors are working together on their own development (see Chapter 8).

Three stories

Your task after each story is to:

- consider and list the messages you can take from the story for your work as a mentor; then
- go to the end of the chapter and compare your list with the messages found by mentors I have worked with.

If you are working through this book with a colleague, you may like to rehearse telling one of the stories to the other and reading one story to yourselves. In this way, you will both have three experiences – telling a story, listening to a story and reading one to yourself. If you choose to tell a story, see 'Telling versus reading stories' below for ideas on how to prepare yourself. (But don't peek at the 'Messages other mentors found' section yet!) If you can do this, you can not only discuss and agree upon your lists of messages, but also note the differing effects, if any, listening to a story being told and reading a story for yourself may have had on you.

Story 1 The Boy and the Cocoon

(Inspired by/adapted from an incident in N. Kazanzakis, 2014.)
One day a boy, who loved nothing better than finding, examining and playing with all kinds of creepy-crawlies, went for a walk in a wood. He came across a cocoon on a sunny tree branch with a very tiny hole in it. He looked very carefully and realised that a butterfly was about to come out. He was so very excited. He took

the cocoon in the palm of his hand and waited. Sure enough, the hole, when he bent to look closely again, seemed slightly bigger. He tried to imagine what kind of butterfly would emerge. Would it be a magnificent 'Red Admiral', a rare 'Blue' or even a disappointing common 'Cabbage white' perhaps? No, not a Cabbage White, he thought, not in the woods. Oh, he was so excited! What a story he would have to tell his friends!

He waited again and peered at the hole. Was it bigger now? He couldn't tell. Perhaps he could help. He leant in and breathed on the cocoon. It worked! His hot breath seemed to be making the hole bigger. He huffed and huffed again until he saw the butterfly beginning to come out of the hole. The more he huffed the quicker the butterfly emerged – until, at last, the whole butterfly was on the palm of his hand trembling and trying to unfurl its wings, next to the empty shell of the cocoon.

But when he looked closely at the pale butterfly, he gasped. He gasped first in disappointment, then in horror and finally with crushing guilt. What was he looking at you ask? He saw first the lack of colour on the butterfly – none at all. Then he noticed the distorted, deformed wings, before watching, with tears running down his cheeks, as the butterfly shuddered and died in the palm of his hand.

Story 2 Mummy Mouse

(Decades ago, as a joke, a version of this story was circulating in the language teacher circles I belonged to. I was reminded of it reading Owen's [2001] 'Lunchtime Learning' story. This is my adapted version.)

In the corner of a meadow on a farm in England, there was a nest of mice. In the nest, Mummy Mouse watched over her babies. She waited patiently, while teaching them other things, for the day their eyes would open, and she could introduce them to the big wide world outside.

The day came. Mummy Mouse ushered her children out of the nest and into the field. One little one seemed reluctant, and Mummy mouse had to nudge him on, murmuring reassuring words. "It's all right, I'll be with you."

Half an hour later, Mummy Mouse, her heart swelling with love and pride, watched as her babies played in the leaves and grass, sniffing new smells and taking in new sights. In the distance she saw her neighbour Mr. Squirrel.

"Good Morning, Mr. Squirrel!" she called out. "Come and meet my children!"

The squirrel came over. The babies stopped playing and hid behind Mummy Mouse. "It's all right, children," said Mummy Mouse. "This is Mr. Squirrel. Say hello!"

"Hello, Mr. Squirrel!" the babies chorused. After a bit of chat, Mr. Squirrel bounded off.

Mummy Mouse turned to her children. "Now then, you've met Mr. Squirrel. Would you recognise him again?"

"Oh yes," they said. "He has a beautiful long and bushy tail."

"Good," said Mummy Mouse, "because not only is he a friend, but where he goes you can often find nuts and tasty things to eat."

The baby mice resumed their playing. The sun was higher in the sky when, all of a sudden, a big shadow came over the mouse family. Mummy Mouse stiffened and looked up into the eyes of Tom, the farm cat. In his eyes, she read only one thing: "Mmmmm, yum, lunch!"

Mummy Mouse thought, "Not *my* babies."

She made sure she was between the cat and her babies, puffed herself up as big as she could, looked up at Tom and made a very strange sound to her children's ears. She *barked* – a very loud bark, just like the farm dog's, Tom's sworn enemy. Now Tom was not very bright and didn't know whether to believe his eyes or his ears. But to be on the safe side, he turned tail and ran away. Whew!

Mummy Mouse turned again to her babies. "Now *he* is our enemy. I'm sorry to say, but he eats mice for his lunch sometimes. Would you recognise him again?"

One baby said, "Oh, yes. He is bigger than Mr. Squirrel."

Another baby said, "And he has whiskers."

Another said, "And his tail is long and thin, not bushy at all."

"Oh, well noticed," said Mummy Mouse. "If I'm not with you and you see him, hide and stay very still."

"But Mummy," began one little baby mouse, "why did you seem to get so big and why did you make such strange sounds?"

"Well," said Mummy Mouse, "I wanted you to have time to look carefully at CAT and to keep you safe, and I wanted you to learn other things, too. What do you think they are?"

The babies were quiet as they thought. Then one baby said tentatively, "Umm, sometimes we may need to be brave?"

Mummy Mouse replied, "Well, yes, that's true. But not until you are grown up!"

Then a second baby shouted triumphantly, "I know! You showed us the importance of learning a foreign language!"

"Well done," said Mummy Mouse. "I think that's enough for now. Let's go back to our nest and have lunch."

So, they did.

Story 3 The Desert Nomads

(This is another story with a long oral tradition. There is also a version in Owen [2001].)

Some nomads were travelling in the desert. They travelled from one oasis to another in order to be able to feed and water themselves and their camels. One night, they unpacked their saddlebags as usual, taking out cooking utensils, food, fire-lighting equipment and sleeping mats and blankets and set about their various evening tasks. Some took charge of the camels, some of the fire and some of the cooking for themselves. Soon, the camels had been fed and watered and were settled down for the night. The nomads, too, had eaten, and in the cold pitch black of the desert night, they were lying on their sleeping mats, covered with their blankets, looking up at a huge sky studded with a myriad of stars. Suddenly, one of them noticed the stars fading from view and a strange growing light in the sky. He alerted the others, and they all stared in amazement. When no more stars could be seen and it was almost as light as day, the nomads cowered fearfully under their blankets. Then, out of the light, there came a voice.

And the voice said, "Go into the desert. Collect pebbles. And tomorrow you will be delighted, disappointed and very, very curious."

And that was it. Nothing else was said. The light gradually disappeared, all was dark again and the stars reappeared.

The nomads were perplexed and murmured amongst themselves. What should they do? Many were loath to get out of their warm blankets to embark on little more than rubbish collecting. Why hadn't they been told something really useful, like how to rescue the planet from global warming, stop wars or cure cancer? Some opted to stay where they were, but a few got up, wandered out to a pebbly path and collected a few handfuls of pebbles which they slung in their saddlebags before going back to bed and to sleep.

The next morning, the nomads packed up their camp and travelled on, over dunes and through rocky valleys to the next oasis. Here, while going about their usual routine setting up camp, one of them noticed something glinting at the bottom of his saddlebag. Tremulously, he reached in a hand and pulled out a pebble that had broken in two during their journey. He looked in astonishment at the raw diamond in the centre of the broken pebble which was glistening in the sunlight. To say he was delighted is somewhat of an understatement. He called the others and excitedly began to pull out the other few pebbles he had collected. So did the others who had some pebbles and one or two also found raw diamonds when they broke the diamonds to look inside. Gradually, they all became rather disappointed that they hadn't collected more. The travellers who hadn't collected any pebbles were especially downcast.

As they talked over dinner, reliving the excitement of discovering the diamonds in seemingly worthless pebbles, one of them wondered, "What if we looked carefully inside more of these ordinary everyday things? We might find more precious gems."

And so, they became very, very curious.

Using allegorical stories in group meetings – telling versus reading stories

There are differences between the experiences of listening to a well-told story, listening to someone else reading a story aloud and reading a story for yourself. For me, the most impactful and memorable are those stories I've heard *told*, with reading them for myself coming second and those someone has read aloud coming a distant third.

If you decide to use an allegorical story in your group, there are therefore two options: give your colleagues a handout with a story to read or tell them the story. In both cases, this can usefully be followed by small groups working with a task eliciting 'messages' similar to the one I set you earlier in this chapter.

Storytelling

Storytellers often use props and different voices to make the stories come alive. Storytelling is a performance art. We are not professional storytellers, but there are things we can do to make our listeners' experiences more memorable and vivid if we choose to *tell* our colleagues an allegorical story.

The most important, I think, is to rehearse the storytelling. I make a skeleton of the story – a list of one or two words for each important part of the story – to glance at if I can't remember what comes next – and I practise. I practise in the mirror and then with anyone I can persuade to listen to my story. I run through the skeleton of the story in my mind before I go to sleep on the night before I am going to tell it and imagine audience reactions and 'what ifs' (see Chapter 6). The aim is to know the story and tell it in your own words, without any paper in hand, in response to and often with the particular audience you are telling it to.

Lastly, you can collect visual aids to support the memorability of the stories you tell. By 'memorability' I mean how easy it is for a listener to remember: the experience of listening to the story; the experience of thinking of its relevance to mentoring and the messages-to-self listeners took from the story. When the experiences are enjoyable, the Undermind of listeners will continue to process them, and perhaps further insights can emerge. The metaphors in the story and the playfulness of toy-like visual aids during the storytelling provide the context for insights to emerge at the time, and the enjoyment (fun) aids recall so that further insights may emerge at a later date (see Chapter 8). At the very least the memory of the experience, however vague, can serve as a reminder of the more important 'messages to self' the listener or group made at the time. My collection, made over many years, includes several items: a plush, cocoon-like caterpillar which can be unzipped and turned inside out to reveal a butterfly (bought in a bring-and-buy sale at the school of one of my sons decades ago); a furry 'Mummy Mouse' hat with ears and eyes (bought because it was colder than I'd expected once in China); and some baby mice finger puppets (bought at the Museum of Modern Art while at a conference in New York). I also have some PowerPoint files with images supporting my telling of various of the stories either for very large groups (as in China) or conference situations.

Commentaries and messages other mentors found

The Boy and the Cocoon

This story illustrates the need for mentors to provide the conditions needed for the new butterfly-teachers to emerge comfortably and at their own pace (for student and beginning-/early-career teachers) and be coloured in their own individually and contextually appropriate ways and fly high and away (for more-experienced mentees). This story has long been a central one in my view of mentoring. It has inspired the cover design of this book.

The 'messages' and reminders mentors have taken from listening to 'The Boy and the Cocoon' have usually centred around the following ideas:

- The need to be patient and allowing the mentee to develop at their own natural pace. Effective mentoring takes time.
- The need to provide appropriate conditions for development – warmth, but not heat.
- The dire consequences of *not* being patient or of *not* ensuring appropriate conditions for development – consequences such as teacher dropout.
- Some groups have linked the boy's behaviour to that of the Shark (see Chapter 8).

Mummy Mouse

The main reason I tell this story is to exemplify all five mentor roles. Did you spot them?

Support: the nudging and reassuring words for the baby who was reluctant to leave the nest

Acculturator: the whole story really, and Mummy Mouse's decision to take her babies out to show them, and get them used to, the big wide world

Model: Mummy Mouse's behaviour towards Mr. Squirrel and Tom

Sponsor: introducing her babies to her friend, the very useful Mr. Squirrel

Educator: asking her babies to tell her what they noticed and letting them work things out for themselves

Mentors have also identified messages to do with:

- being brave for your mentee's sake, for example, the possible need to protect a mentee from those who might do them harm in the context (see Chapter 1); or
- language learning – in the sense of learning the jargon that marks people out as belonging to particular professional cultures (see Chapter 3).

The Desert Nomads

The main reason I tell this story is related to noticing. Sometimes (depending on my audience and the context) I conclude with something like "so go collect those noticing pebbles, notice the ordinary things in your classrooms and look very closely (using the SIRP tool to help you do so), and you *will* find precious gems!"

The messages mentors take away, as well as being related to noticing and the finding of important gems of understanding from looking closely at ordinary things, are usually linked to the initial challenges of using SIRP (see Chapter 6). Two examples:

- Once the first use of SIRP has reached a satisfying conclusion for the mentee – gems have been found – it will get easier to encourage mentees to develop their noticing – pick up more noticing pebbles – and follow the structure of the SIRP protocol.
- Trust the process – do what 'the voice' says.

In the next and concluding chapter, I highlight some of the ideas presented in the book as they might be relevant to various types of readers. I also present three professional stories to illustrate the benefits to you that becoming, being and developing as a mentor can bring.

References

Elbaz, F. (1991), Research on teacher's knowledge: the evolution of a discourse. *Journal of Curriculum Studies*, Vol. 23, No. 1, pp.1–19.

Kazantzakis, N. (2014), *Zorba the Greek: the saint's life of Alexis Zorba*. New York: Simon and Schuster, first published 1946.

Owen, N. (2001), *The magic of metaphor: 77 stories for teachers, trainers and thinkers*. Carmarthen: Crown House.

10 Conclusions

One of my main aims in writing this book was to describe processes and practices which allow mentors to remain ONSIDE and avoid judgementoring. This allows mentors to support mentees' learning and wellbeing in ways which, in turn, contribute to teacher retention in the profession.

I also aimed to make the book relevant and useful to all mentors of teachers whatever their context, and, for example, describe ways individual practices or processes can be adjusted according to context.

In this concluding chapter, the first section attempts to highlight aspects of the book that I see as particularly relevant to various types of readers, reprising a theme from the Introduction. I start by considering mentors of two different broad categories of mentee before turning to external and online mentoring which, in certain contexts and circumstances, is the only mode of working possible for many mentors of both types. I then summarise some of what I hope other ToTs might have found useful in this text.

The final section contains some personal/professional stories of people who have become mentors or undertaken mentor courses. This is to illustrate the possible impact of mentoring on mentors' (and ToTs') own development and careers, suggest possible developments in the field of mentoring and perhaps motivate those beginning-mentor readers for whom the hard work of adding mentoring to their already very demanding teaching job may, initially at least, feel rather thankless.

How the book might be relevant to different readers

Mentors of student and beginning teachers

These mentors are not only the most numerous but, it seems to me, also currently have the most demanding task for two main reasons.

Firstly, it is the mentors of student or beginning teachers who most often find themselves in contexts where it is expected that they fulfil the additional duties of trainer and/or assessor. The book attempts to support such mentors in doing so without too many negative effects on that relationship and while making mentoring and the individual mentee's learning pathway central.

Secondly, as such mentees are at the early stages of teacher learning, they very often want and expect to be told what to do and whether what they are doing is 'right' or 'wrong.' Mentors need to find ways not only to explain to and persuade

DOI: 10.4324/9781003429005-11

mentees that this is not a good idea, but also, crucially (and, in my experience, the tougher task), to fight their own experientially learnt instincts to give in and tell them! I do hope this book has given you some rational ammunition for this fight, a rationale for why it is important that you work non-judgementally, as well as the desire to develop the skills that this approach requires.

Mentors of qualified and in-service teachers

In England, early-career teachers (ECTs) are supported for two years by a timetable reduction (10% in the first year and 5% in the second). A mentor is assigned to support the ECTs in working towards achieving the general teaching standards via a process set out by the Early Career Framework (DfE 2019). Formal training, aimed towards helping ECTs achieve the eight 'standards' for this phase of their professional development, is also available. Research was carried out after the first year of the first rollout of this scheme (Institute for Employment Studies and BMG Research, 2022). ECTs were asked a number of questions, including one about their hopes for the mentoring process. ECTs reported 'hoping to improve their skills in adaptive teaching.' (As an aside, I think this term is tautological in that all teaching, understood as supporting learning, must inevitably be adaptive and cater to the needs of the particular group of students. On the other hand, perhaps stressing the need to be responsive to student needs through the use of this term helps overcome any residual 'teaching-as-telling' notions.) The response given by the highest number of ECTs to the question about their hopes for the mentoring process was 'receiving constructive and non-judgemental guidance and support.' Mentor training, in various formats including blended, with some face-to-face and some online, is also provided. But the report identifies problems with this approach, including the familiar one of a too-heavy workload for mentors to engage in this training. If you are a mentor in such a scheme, whether in England or elsewhere, I believe this book can be of help to you in supporting your mentees to realise their hopes, filling in any gaps caused by missed training sessions, and perhaps in lobbying for sufficient time, not only to mentor, but also to engage in your own development for this crucial role as a mentor.

Mentees in this broad category of qualified teachers also include people who are new to your school, but experienced colleagues. With these mentees, the Acculturator role may be foregrounded, at least initially, before your colleague is inducted, so to speak, into a further feature of your community – one in which peer-supported SIRP is a norm and where having a "slurp and SIRP" session over coffee (slirping?!) is a frequent and legitimate activity. In addition, mentoring may be offered to any/all colleagues in contexts where, for example, reforms are being introduced and all colleagues see the need for support in adapting their practices. Another situation is where those in charge of staff development (perhaps organised to fix any assessor's perceptions of widespread deficits) have realised that a one-size-fits-all training or development programme is not achieving the desired effects. In such situations, a voluntary peer-mentoring scheme, open to all staff, can be implemented, where pairs of colleagues agree to work together taking turns in undertaking the mentor and mentee roles. In this situation, it is important that 'management' supports and acknowledges participants – whether or not those that it is thought most need 'fixing' are participating, and whether or not it may seem, at any given point, that the mentoring is in fact 'fixing' anything. Apart from the fact that mentoring takes time, if participation is favourably viewed, others will want to volunteer and participate, too. This is important. Some of the dangers of requiring the 'poor' teachers to become mentees are discussed in the next section. I believe that *all* teachers benefit from time spent in their careers as mentees, and that any local professional community benefits from having a mentoring programme in place.

For mentors working with qualified colleagues, the non-judgemental approach described throughout this book is ideal.

External and online mentors

The approach described in this book is very suited to the work of external mentors, too, whoever the mentees might be. External mentor-readers will have needed to select from those activities they *can* do and identify those that, because they are not part of the same school or institutional community and present on a daily basis, they cannot. However, although being an external mentor or having to work online can be a disadvantage, particularly in the local Acculturator role and in some aspects of the Sponsor role, it may also be advantageous in some contexts. I know of two situations where this is the case. The first is where the mentee is in a small school, and they are the only teacher of a particular subject, so a mentor-teacher of the same subject in another school undertakes the role. The second sad situation was where in-service 'mentoring' – in the form of judgementoring – had unfortunately become associated with being needed only by 'bad' or 'failing' teachers. Having an external 'outsider' mentor was an advantage in that it allowed mentees to keep their mentoring private and thus save face.

Much external mentoring is carried out online, and the approach described in the book is particularly suited to this. In the recent pandemic, for example, many school-based mentors were also working online. Whether or not the teaching is also happening online does not affect this work. As the mentor does not observe teaching of whatever kind as a regular practice, the SIRP protocol, for example, can just as easily be used in video calls to guide the mentee's thinking and learning. However, I do believe that relationship-building, for example, is best done face-to-face. While some may think this belief marks me as 'old-school', many colleagues now share this belief after the experiences of so much 'zooming' during the pandemic.

As an aside, one of my draft readers, on reading the previous sentence, wrote a note to confirm that publications now exist suggesting that online communication is indeed a depleted form of communication, and that 'Zoom fatigue' exists. So, I'm not old-school then! As I am not currently a mentor, external or otherwise, I have not read all – well, *any* – of the publications on the four-page list she also sent. I cannot therefore suggest just one that might be useful to read, but I'm hoping it helps just to know they are out there.

Anyway, where face-to-face mentoring is not possible as a regular practice, some external mentors I know have benefitted from ensuring that at least the starting relationship phase (getting to know you and first meetings, see Support role) is conducted face-to-face.

Other ToTs

The approach described in this book is one that distinguishes mentors from other types of ToTs in several ways, for example by what type of teacher knowledge is learnt (see Introduction). Lecturers, trainers and tutors might take heart from the knowledge that their work is made relevant and useful to their students by the work of a mentor. With the help of a mentor who works in the ways described in this book, your work can have real-world impact.

One main and crucial difference between other ToTs and mentors is that, in mentoring, it is the mentee who decides what is to be learnt (the curriculum) and when (the pace and timing). Allowing the mentee agency in this way increases a mentee's self-confidence and satisfaction and supports the development of their learnacy. This is possible in the one-to-one mentoring relationship, one which makes congruent, scaffolded learning achievable. Most other ToTs do not have this possibility. So, for me, if you are working with groups of learners and make the decisions about what those learners *should* learn, or should learn next, you are not a mentor. You may be able, however, to take a mentoring *approach* to your work. You can elicit and work with your learners' goals, for example, and enact some mentor roles – perhaps for the whole group in Sponsor role, or for one group member who seeks you out in the Support role. One of my readers suggested that, simply put, a ToT who genuinely cares about their learners as people and who cares about their *learning* could be said to be taking a mentoring approach.

Other ToTs choosing to read this book are most likely to be working with formal teacher education programmes. They probably have some formal relationship with the mentoring strand of the programme where there is one, and they may be charged with setting up mentoring schemes, preparing teachers to become mentors or interacting with the mentors of their students. I hope this book will have painted a detailed picture of what effective mentoring can look like and so stimulated thoughts and actions on how to enact their own roles in ways which allow mentors to achieve the powerful potential benefits of mentoring – supporting mentees' learning and wellbeing which, in turn, contribute to teacher retention.

What's in it for you

I wrote above that many mentors can feel, at least at the start of the work, that mentoring is rather a thankless task. Most mentors I know are expected to undertake the mentoring role alongside full-time teaching, often with insufficient time to mentor or develop as a mentor, and they receive little or no extra financial gain. Some gain a certain local status and recognition. For some, their mentoring work has contributed eventually to a higher grade and pay increase. However, it may seem at first as though becoming a mentor involves a lot of extra work for little obvious reward. Yet most mentors who have committed to their development and work as mentors report a renewed enthusiasm for teaching and positive impacts on both their personal and professional lives.

So, to readers adopting the approach described in this book, I want to say that you will be rewarded by your own and your mentees' satisfaction and the knowledge that you are not only supporting the development of your mentees but also of yourself and the whole teaching profession. You may also be rewarded by – perhaps initially unexpected – developments in your own career, too, as the stories below illustrate. The people who sent these stories are not a 'representative sample', they are friends and colleagues, who very kindly agreed to send me their stories (see Acknowledgements). There is also more formal research-based corroboration for the positive benefits on the mentors themselves, including in Bodòczky and Malderez (1997).

Anna's story

This first story is from a currently practising school-based mentor for student and early-career teachers. She writes in her covering email, "Really, it is all thanks to the mentor course, I would not have had any of the benefits below were it not for the course." I happen to know that she is also now involved in mentor training, too.

> How to share my passion for teaching? I first became interested in mentoring because I wanted to share this passion, but did not know how to. Learning mentoring has not only given me the tools to be able to support colleagues or future colleagues, it has also kept me on my toes to be on the lookout for innovative ideas, for opportunities to grow professionally.

Thanks to mentoring, I am constantly in touch with young people entering the profession, bringing their own perspectives and worldview to teaching. Now I understand that our profession progresses best if there is a constant dialogue between teachers as opposed to certainties handed down or acquired individually and written in stone. Engaging in this dialogue has helped me become more reflective of my own teaching and has given me the sense of being an active member of a larger professional community. I used to think that I would be mentoring to support others, but in fact, mentoring has supported me in my career just as much. In the process, I like to think that I have become a better listener, and, therefore, a better person.

Doina's story

This second story was a bit longer than the 200 to 300 words I was expecting! As it is from a friend and colleague who has been in mentoring almost as long as I have, this is hardly surprising. I give it in full here.

I need to give a bit of background to explain aspects of the first paragraph. The mentor course format that Doina and many others followed at that time ran concurrently with a normal teaching timetable. Typically, teachers-becoming-mentors in that part of the world at that time attended a weekly session that was 3 or more hours long and took place on Fridays from late afternoon into early evening and/or on Saturdays. They also often had weeklong intensive meetings during the school holidays, for a total of about 120 hours. Early courses were projects run by the British Council, while participants paid for later ones. All participants attended voluntarily.

> When I started a mentoring course my personal and professional life took a significant turn. Slowly but surely, I become aware that my relationship[s] with the members of my family, with my students and my colleagues were warmer and more meaningful. My son, who was a teenager at that time, got closer and more open to me and it was obvious to me that he trusted me more and even accepted my opinions and suggestions a lot more easily than before.
>
> One student actually said to me one day: "Teacher, you have changed! You remain positive when responding to negative students or their contributions." That remark made my day (and my life, for that matter). I realized then that my teaching behaviour had in fact changed for the better.
>
> I had been a reflective teacher before, but now I was reflecting in a more structured way and even started reflecting on my classes with a colleague. It worked beautifully for me and more colleagues started asking me to work with them too. They appreciated what they said was the constructive and non-judgemental way we worked.

My status in my school and among my fellow mentors, with whom I kept in permanent contact, changed as well and we all came to the conclusion that what we were doing in our respective schools with the student teachers and the beginner teachers really made a positive difference. It was with this realisation that the idea of setting up a mentor association came into discussion. We were convinced that in that way we would gain a stronger voice and would be able to bring about a significant change in the way student-teachers were prepared for their job and how professional development was seen in our educational system. The National Association of Romanian Mentors was born in 2007 and I was one of its first Presidents. We were consulted by the Ministry of Education and after I'd had several meetings with 2–3 ministers a decision was taken and they changed the law and introduced a new qualification: school-based mentor for beginner teachers. This recognised the status of such mentors. About 85% of our comments on the draft bill were taken on board.

Around the same time, I took a further two-week summer course to become a mentor trainer, and worked on about 100 courses preparing more that 3000 of colleagues for mentoring all over the world. More than 2000 were in Romania. Mentor training also took me to Uzbekistan, Chile and Kenya.

When it was time to retire from my full-time state school teaching post, I did not really retire. Having become more and more confident in planning my own professional path, my professional journey continued. I became an e-moderator [Author's note: an online ToT]. My mentoring skills were noticed and I have been asked to mentor e-moderators from different countries (Morocco, Palestine, Libya, UK, Spain, Mexico). I am now a 'recognised' specialist in this field of education that has given me the chance to experience professional achievement and success.

I owe the opportunity to live all these wonderful professional experiences to the decision over 25 years ago to do a mentor course and become a trained mentor.

Elena's story

Next and finally comes a story from a ToT friend, former student and mentee and mentor course attendee, and someone who has in many respects been my mentor during this long book-producing process. She works in a context where formal teacher preparation prioritises KA development with some work on KH and where partnerships with mentors in schools are just in the process of being established.

I work as a teacher educator at a university in North Macedonia, supporting the development of pre-service English language teachers (in this text: 'students'). Having experienced the benefits of SIRP as a mentee, I was convinced of its affordances for my students. I adopted the SIRP framework to structure our discussion sessions following classroom observation in order to move away from our impressionistic discussions thus far, e.g. by sharing what we may have appreciated or not in a lesson, or how to 'fix' a problem. Instead of rushing into conclusions, we now took time to study and better understand a classroom episode of my students' choice, hypothesise about what might have brought it about and consider relevant literature in order to arrive at informed conclusions. Once students get used to the model, they engage in peer mentoring, which they particularly enjoy for its more personal nature.

I have found using SIRP to be an implicit way to raise awareness about the importance of noticing in education. Developing a 'love of data' results in my students creating intricate learner data sets on which to base their instructional decisions; this, for me, captures the essence of teaching. The students are regularly taken aback by the many possible explanations for a single teaching event – another instance of SIRP implicitly bringing to their attention the centrality of context in teaching. Another 'a-ha' moment for my students is realising the usefulness of theory, i.e. its potential to inform practical teaching decisions. I hope that our exercises in SIRP will give my students a flavour of the habit of regular professional reflection, and a passion to continue developing their skills beyond their formal studies.

Using SIRP with my students has had benefits for my own professional development, too: some of my students' insights have made me think and research in directions I would not have otherwise considered.

I hope the stories above have shown some of the ways becoming and being a mentor or involvement with mentoring can benefit not only the profession but you, personally, too.

There is food for thought, I imagine, for all of us on reading the stories above. But here, at the end of the book, I'd like to pick up on the idea of a formal 'mentor association' to increase professionalism. I have heard mentors referred to as 'new training professionals' but wonder if they are or even can be fully professional in many contexts (see Chapter 4 for a full list of things that professionals are or do, in my view). Perhaps one day you could start or contribute to a teacher mentor association?!

Towards an ending

This book has, deliberately, proposed just one way of understanding what mentoring is and described what could be seen as a 'starter set' of practices and processes to enact ONSIDE mentoring. This is in order to be of immediate practical use to teachers becoming mentors and practising mentors as well as, perhaps, to challenge some established, taken-for granted views and practices. It is not offered as 'right' or definitive. It is, however, one of the only approaches to date that I know of which helps mentors actively avoid judgementoring and remain ONSIDE, and it has been extensively trialled in a variety of contexts. My hope is that it can be a starting point for new mentors and, for practising mentors, a stepping stone on an absorbing and very rewarding learning-mentoring journey.

Finally, I'd like to thank you for reading this book, for the inspiration you have given me to write it and, most of all, for the work you do. I wish you many instances of 'flow' (see Chapter 8), fun and satisfaction as you continue learning, developing and advocating for effective mentoring and the conditions that support it.

References

Bodòczky, C. & Malderez, A. (1997), The INSET impact of a mentoring course. In D. Hayes (Ed.) *In-service teacher development: international perspectives.* Hemel Hempstead: Prentice Hall. Accessed at: https://doi.org/10.1016/j.tate.2008.09.001

Early Career Framework. (2019), *DfE.* Accessed February 2023 at: https://assets.publishing.service.gov.uk/government/uploads/system/uploads/attachment_data/file/978358/Early-Career_Framework_April_2021.pdf

Institute for Employment Studies and BMG Research. (2022), *Evaluation of the national roll-out of the early career framework induction programmes interim research brief (year one).* DfE. Accessed February 2023 at: https://assets.publishing.service.gov.uk/government/uploads/system/uploads/attachment_data/file/1078234/ECF_evaluation_interim_research_brief_2022.pdf

Appendix: Core mentor standards

- A mentor is a professional teacher who is approachable, patient and willing to learn and to make time for a mentee.
- A mentor uses their knowledge and skills (expressed briefly in the table below) appropriately to support each individual mentee's wellbeing and learning.
- Any one mentor, depending on context, may be expected to also fulfil trainer standards and/or assessor standards (not given here).

Using the five roles of mentoring, the table below sets out what mentors understand and know how to do.

In Support role, understands that...	In Support role, knows how to...
A good mentor-mentee relationship is fundamental.	Start, maintain and end a productive relationship.
Good relationships are trusting and safe.	Build trust and maintain confidentiality.
Learning teaching can be an emotional roller coaster.	Actively listen to stand-under (empathise with) and to understand (learn more about) a mentee.
We need to understand learners in order to scaffold appropriately.	
There may be rare times when doing things *for* a mentee can be appropriate.	Offer a suggestion or an extra pair of hands at times and in ways that do not compromise work in the Educator role.
In Acculturator role, understands that...	**In Acculturator role, knows how to...**
All professional communities have their own norms, languages and practices which, for a mentor as a member of those communities, will have become unremarkable.	Remember what it felt like to arrive in the communities and point out important features.
Every community member contributes to its culture.	Involve the mentee in all community activities and value their contributions.

(Continued)

(Continued)

In Acculturator role, understands that...	In Acculturator role, knows how to...
Belonging to a professional association is part of becoming a professional.	Find ways to include their mentee in their own professional association activities.
In Model role, understands that...	**In Model role, knows how to...**
A mentor models a way of being as a teacher, their professionalism (rather than their teaching or a way to teach, for example).	Ensure they are indeed engaged in all aspects of being a professional.
There are many aspects of professionalism that are usually private and invisible to others.	Make the invisible aspects of their professionalism visible to their mentee.
In Sponsor role, understands that...	**In Sponsor role, knows how to...**
A mentor uses any power they have (from their knowledge and contacts) in the service of the mentee.	Use their knowledge and contacts appropriately to enhance their mentee's learning and wellbeing.
In Educator role, understands that...	**In Educator role, knows how to...**
A mentor remains non-judgmental.	Work to ensure that any processes, practices and protocols they use enable them to ensure that it is the mentees themselves who make any judgements or plans.
Teachers say they learn best 'from experience.'	Use protocols which enable teachers to learn from their own and others' experiences.
Professional teachers are reflective practitioners, and reflective practice needs to be learnt.	Use protocols which enable the learning of informed reflective practice.
This is a largely a listening role.	Actively listen as their mentee works through the scaffolded steps of the process of learning from experience, contributing their ideas only on invitation.
It is the pupils who provide invaluable feedback to the mentee – if they notice it.	Actively listen (to get a clear picture of what happened and support the development of the mentee's noticing) at the start of the learning from experience process.

Index

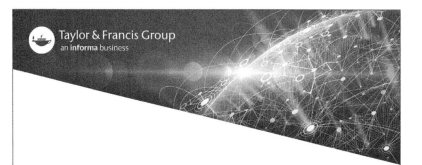

Printed and bound by CPI Group (UK) Ltd, Croydon, CR0 4YY

09/08/2024

01024941-0016